FUCK ISOLATION:
a Tribute
to the
COVID-19 Experience

GARDEN OAK PRESS
Rainbow, California

Garden Oak Press
1953 Huffstatler St., Suite A
Rainbow, CA 92028
(760) 728-2088
gardenoakpress.com
gardenoakpress@gmail.com

First published by Garden Oak Press on June 25, 2020

ISBN-13: 978-1-7350556-1-9

Printed in the United States of America

The views expressed in this anthology of poems are solely those
of the poets and do not necessarily reflect the views of the
Publisher, and the Publisher hereby disclaims any responsibility for
them.

FUCK ISOLATION:
a Tribute
to the
COVID-19 Experience

Editors

HAYLI NICOLE

SUNNY REY

Art Director

AUBREE MILLER

CONTENTS

A NOTE FROM ONE OF OUR EDITORS

Poets Underground has played a vital role in my healing journey and has allowed me to support so many others in theirs. My goal in life is to help people tell their stories and publish their first body of work. Today, we have a wealth of new voices speaking to their unique experience that will now live on the same shelves as the people who inspired us to be writers. There is nothing more powerful than following in the footsteps of our ancestors, our leaders, our idols, and our muses. May this anthology be the first opened door of many on your creative journey as well as the invitation for others to believe they are worthy of the same.

My sincerest thank you to Sunny, Aubree, and Bill for letting me be a part of the creation of this anthology. It is with great responsibility and pride that I got to be a small part of its completion. The hours of collective energy dedicated to ensuring so many diverse voices be heard during a significant time in our lived history will forever be one of the greatest accomplishments. To the Poets Underground community and contributors beyond our creative family, a million times thank you for trusting us with your words and giving us the opportunity to share your experience with others. I look forward to the day a person holds this anthology in their hands and recognizes your experience as a parallel of their own despite the implications of a global pandemic. Let this collection be a reminder of the infinite threads in our collective humanity. This anthology truly embodies the interconnectedness of our lived experience. It serves as proof that community is stronger than adversity and I feel so grateful to have been a piece of the creative journey.

— HAYLI NICOLE

Morning Walk

While fear ensnares us
Birds remember it is Spring
Children draw chalk hearts

— KAREN KENYON

Mourning
What Was

3

Mourning
What Was

The Spring of Our Discontent

JENNIFER MCBROOM

In 10 years,
we'll tell our kids
about the coldest
spring where only
fear bloomed.

Going into Lockdown

LISE BREAKEY

Breathe.
There is
mesquite honey
palo verde blossom
the desert's warm rain.
God's love
smells like this.

I cultivate gratitude
but there is
blight
early frost
crop failure.
Come winter
gleanings must suffice:

a starving man's feast
the memory of a ruby
your presence in my dreams
your ghost around the corner.

I hope it will be enough that I had
warm rain and mesquite honey.

Home-schooled by a Virus

ADVERSARY

Altered; without apathy
Questions stirring of what's to come
As we pick up the pieces of a shattered image or a beautiful memory;
that once was whole.
The corners become tattered,
They start to display that time is real
They peal back a little bit,
       exposing the multiple layers that exist within,
Hidden from the naked eye
Yet, limiting it to be able to fit together in a way it once did.
We try to replace what we have lost
Maybe by looking around for different pieces
                that could possibly click into place
Ones that are similarly shaped
but they don't.
Even when you know deep below the surface that there's something
missing, something that has been broken,
There's nothing to fill that void
No forward progression
Feeding the flame with premium gasoline,
not water
its human nature,
When shouting at the sky can lead to an avalanche, of regret
In certain instances,
when something has died, there will never be a replacement
No vacancy
Only anguish

Exponent

FLYGIRL_REE

I cried over you today
Thought of you
It made my grey
To stress
Oh, Lord knows what came next

Things unseen
Words he would never mean
I cried over you today
Thought of you
It made my hair grey

Flickering Dream

WILLIAM MOHOFF JR.

How I recall the sun kissing my face,
how the wind danced with me and how the flowers bowed,
merriment and laughter heard from the bird's tongues
                                    soaring high like my love
Four walls protect me from the outside world,
but they don't protect me from myself
I'm plagued by my thoughts and no one to share them with
They manifest into beings that linger over me
I share cups of coffee with sorrow and lay in bed with regret
I pass my time conversing with sadness
                          and am ignored by happiness
How is it that my place of retreat is now my tomb that I can't leave.

Casualty List

DR. LEWIS KRUGLICK

Night is worse

when it comes in daylight;
not dressed in darkness
but hung with the festival
lanterns of unseen beasts.

They cavort through the body.
They plunder the host.
A delirium of fever
steals breath from the chest.

They cough up confusion
and slip through defenses,
while their victims of mayhem
are stacked in cold storage.

Time to put the mark
of blood on the doorstep
in hope that the Angel
of death will ignore you.
Passover – Passover.

And still the casualty list
keeps growing.

The Crown

JASON NOBLE

There is a pox amongst us
It sits
It stinks
It smiles
It smells
You can feel it
You can taste it
You can't quite touch it
but it is there
It is yours
It is mine
It is ours
It's Those things I did
Those things you did
Those things we all done did
It lives down there and hides
In the teenage basement playrooms
Where our remorse and our regrets reside
It slithers and wiggles and wriggles inside
And in a satanic blood orgy we dance
And with our darkest secrets we slide
Those secrets which we carry to our grave
And tell no one
Not lovers
Not family
Not friends
Not even on a suicide note
On a tightened noose
Friday night
Means to a fucking end
Limitless despair and anxiety
Sadness and Melancholy
Rule this guilt riddled throne
We wear this crown under a threat of sickness
It's invisible yet palpable
In Isolation
In Quarantine
Sheltered in place
This thing
It crushes you
It smothers you

Like an unwanted senior prom slow dance
Or a heavy sword wielded with expert arms
It doesn't need to be sharp
The weight alone when swung properly will crush your skull
Hopeless fantasies
Cathartic lethargy
Cooking, drinking, excessive masturbation
Watching and streaming until your eyeballs dry up
Like sand in a never ending hourglass
Except it doesn't tell you what day it is
There is only today, yesterday, and tomorrow
Skin on knuckles cracked and dried
From hands repeatedly washed and sanitized
We wait silently for a check that may never come
While the billionaire's laugh and dance
And eat caviar and sip champagne
On their starline learjets that streak across empty night skies
On the way to their mansion on the hill
Of their private Caribbean Island
All while the stock market crumbles
Only to be born again
Like a zombie Jesus Easter that we all missed
Like a rocket into record breaking territory
Amongst rampant unemployment
And the suffering of the average and the poor
Who wait for a measly $1,200 handout
Or an untraceable unemployment check
While we eat cake
And wish the guillotine would sing its revolutionary song
And the pitchfork torches would once again march the streets
To eat the rich
When will it all end?
I don't know
You don't know
No one fucking knows
Forget sports
Forget shows
Forget the fucking bar
Maybe one day we will see each other again
From
six
feet
Afar

Unexpected Expectations

CRYSTAL BRANDAN

Mind never quiet
No good reason to deny it

Inside wanting out
This new order and making me doubt

Doubt my value my worth
Questioning daily my place on earth

Social gatherings gave me purpose
Now every day feeling worthless

Although I love being alone
This loneliness is one I've never known

This solitude has no answer
Every passing day is a blur

This time has shown me my reality
Maybe time to get out of this fucking city

That's something I expected
Just not realizing my dreams I've neglected

I know I'll see what I have here
Constantly staying out of fear

Searing the community I couldn't let go
Now it seems it was all for show

I think I can move forward now
This time alone has shown me how

Call it a blessing in disguise
I'm sure my leaving won't be a surprise

If it is I hope you wish me well
If you don't you can go straight to hell

Now That I Have Time to Write

JOAN GERSTEIN

Metaphors have departed on insomnia's train.
Similes stay quarantined in someone else's brain.

I can't finagle figures good for poem or speech.
Personification, persona appear beyond my reach.

My shape poems and prose poems are riddled with clichés.
My funny, rhyming narratives, to others, sound passé.

Villanelles and fond rondeaus have lost their refrains.
All my fibs and limericks aren't silly, just inane.

I tried acrostic but forgot what letters I must use.
Lately I fear my mind's hiding in my caboose.

I find on my computer that my found poem stays lost.
My verses miss the meters you see in those of Frost.

Could I, like William Shakespeare, pen some sweet sonnet,
I'd cease all activities and surely pounce upon it,

or emulate Emily who took verse and set it free,
I'd curse worse than Scarlett prattling fiddle-de-dee.

Iambic pentameter, odes, haikus all make me blue,
only because my muse is self-isolating too.

Tree Felling Cuts

NIKO SWAN

A tree falls onto a blue car
Covers the red car in front of it
      Like a skirt
      Like the curtains they put in between surgery and a human
Forget about the unnatural invasive method
And remember a numb blankness

This fallen tree
Reminds me that embrace
Can be painful
      Glass cracks
Splintering across the windshield
      The hard bark of the tree
Resting, now softly in the dent it created upon first impact

I want to remember
The pain that comes with touch
Because now
The pain that comes with the absence
Leaves an aching and invisible scar
Empty space
Of a bruise that never comes to the surface

I want to remember
The beauty of the sunset
Vibrant orange that spills onto my face
And especially Vanessa's
      In the photo we take
Before the gray covers it

But I want to remember the gray
Most of all
What it means to lose
And how far it might be
The distance between me and myself

Encompassed in gray
Hidden underneath the skirt of leaves
It is easy to forget
How the tree fell
With such force
Striking a blue car
And sheltering a red one. Would we call this embrace?

In your arms
All I could remember
Was the first strike
An invisible bruise
That you pushed your strong fingers into
Without asking
Still
A small part of you
Rests, softly in the rawness created upon first impact
Almost an innocent affair
If you could forget the metal knife across my skin
Behind the curtain

Midnight

JAKE ROGERS

ticking down the dim horizon –
volcanos tremble at the thought –
a silence so relentless
the old ghosts all go off howling
skylit oblivion ballads
until marigolds can grow again –

there is no one cliff to walk off – just the steep
steep curling of the Earth's sad history
back and back into dusk –

Need a Title for This Shit

ADVERSARY

Turn down the music
Shut the car, off
Loosen the grip on the steering wheel,
Slow down your thoughts, walk
Freeze them in time before they can, rot;
rot
  rot
    Rot away into the emptiness of your consciousness
Move past the objects in your path that drive you to the haunted
abyss
That place where sunlight does not exist
Where the friends of black holes have an abundance of doubt
to cloud your bliss
I see no windows here
There are no doors
No life
No happiness
Only the ground and the walls are present.
The porcelain tile floor is cold and bleak
As toes curl with every step, they won't let me get cold feet
I cannot leave.
Work here is strictly graveyard shifts
Pulling teeth with bleeding fingertips
Where insanity is a cure to what the shadows diagnosed you with
I struggle to sleep
I seek for a companion
For my soul;
For it is beat.
But hope survives
and there is hope.
Even when all you want to do is drive off a cliff into the sunset,
Forgetting about all your problems
        all your burdens
    Bury yourself in that dark place
you cannot.

There is no magical road you can drive down,
                        that makes all your stress
and fears disappear
So let that dark place only be a mirage in the distance;
not a home.
        Say goodbye to that ride, pause
        Shout to the shadows, mock
        Keys in the ignition, lost.

Sitting with your silence

WILLIAM MOHOFF, JR.

I have forgotten how to speak
This isolation that I woke up in doesn't feel right
I don't remember being in this state
let alone even recall what my life was prior
Every room feels dull and so does my face
each mirror showing me a face I haven't seen before,
strangers inhabiting my space
The outside is haunted with fear
Streets infected with invisible death
Places of gathering now whistle tunes of solitude
Church bells dare not ring
The world now is a vacuum no sounds will be heard or remembered
all we look to now is when we sleep, when we wake,
when we have that moment to sit with our silence and contemplate
whether or not to end it now or just move on.

Collecting Dimes

Niko Swan

S o l i t u d e
    Feels like a treasure
I pick it up
    When I have spent
        All my dimes
    On connection
    Or speaking
        To an empty room
The echoes of my voice
    Sounds like
a conversation
a quiet murmur
"W h a t ? "
    Repeated over
        And over
It is hard to find a room
    Quiet enough
        To hear myself think

What Falls Will Rise

DANNY J MARINO

When sirens break the silence
Morning, noon, and night
It reminds us all that death
In a moment, can take life

Stricken with isolation
In the depths of a lonely heart
Our minds drift off to wander
While the world we know falls apart

Look what the future has come to
The human race inside a cage
Domesticated prisoners
What cruel debt have we paid?

Many of us grow weary
From a dark, unshakeable haze
Millions who lost their jobs
Now aimless, float through the day

On my knees I ask God for His will
For our ancestors' strength and guidance
Protect us from sickness and death
Heal us in stillness & silence

Tempted by fear and weakness
Idle hands, anguish and rage
I propose a new sense of self
Create life from all that remains

Used to It

Angela Murrell

You ever just think
"I'm used to it"?
you ever just sink
into your couch
at the end of a long day
and feel the complacency of it?

You ever feel the guilt
not to have too much fun
cause that's not what should get done?

It's better to play passively
choose a vice, any device,
from couch to bed,
you carry this dread.

You ever seem to feel
tethered to a routine -
like a mental quarantine,
the open space for change and hope
impeded by the need to cope?

You ever notice
the overwhelming burden
of a restrictive attitude -
a deliberate inhibition of self-action,
an idea that we only deserve distraction?

You ever really want
what someone else was brave enough to get
and before you even start, you quit?

You ever ask yourself
if there are things you do to find joy
truly rooted in a plan you devise and deploy?

You ever think that maybe
you should not just be "used to it" -
If you stop making the same old movements
you'd have room for self-improvement?

You ever notice
the trick to forming a habit
is all about repetition -
that this self-doubt inhibition
is a learned behavior that can be overridden
by building better habits that were once forbidden,
as long as you can stay committed to trying
long enough, of course, to get used to it.

Time Above the Clouds

MARJORIE PEZZOLI

Each staying within the confines
of their own bubble tries to find
a way to float above the clouds

Separated from others
my time up here is giving
me fresh perspective

I look forward to the day
when I can rain down
join the occan
frolic in the waves
& swim with everyone

surviving the demands of
an inhospitable environment
(just like bears)

PERI GOOD

clearly
we are not in hibernation
an understandable
mistaken observation
we have gone to sleep
deep within our caves
just like bears
sometimes a touch
or a loud noise
fails to wake us

intent on surviving
energy expenditure minimizing
in here
adapting to the inhospitable
out there
just like bears
temperatures set lower
our heart rates slower
suspended animation
not hibernation
but torpor

we will emerge
eventually
from this involuntary state
of utter inactivity
as conditions dictate
focused, grouchy, wary
ready to eat what spring offers
not thin like bears though
as we have not suppressed
our feeding behaviors

Zombie Apocalypse

DEBORAH RAMOS

Sitting in my solace,
the virus triggers another
malady deep within me.
Mutant tentacles constrict my muse.
Why am I not inspired by this new bug? This tweaked reality?
While poets are submitting
        to the abundance of COVID anthologies,
I am creatively stunned. I can't focus.
It's like I have Super Adult ADD.
I'm not reading or painting. I'm barely writing.
My colors shift to shades of gray.
I need to walk, and shake out the restless legs.
But I'll drive to Von's, making sure
I have plenty of wine and shots of Irish whiskey.
I watch Netflix, Hulu, and reruns of the Wendy Williams Show.
What the fuck is up with that!?
I'm living in sweatpants and the purple slippers
my granddaughter got me for Christmas.
I joined three Zoom open mics so far.
Computer camera is hideously too close to my face,
so I blocked my video when I read.
I sit outside with the cats to steal a beam of sunlight.
We stress eat in solidarity and our waistlines expand together.
Hummingbirds flaunt their freedom
and sip nectar from the sweeping butterfly bush.
No social distancing in the sky.
Tethered to the earth, I dream with envy.

20 by 15

PORTIA REILLY

Self-isolating requires practiced patience:
mornings over coffee, digital checking
on friends
    Why aren't they being more careful?
paperless news from the New York Times:
trustworthy reporting is a gift in this time.

Days on end of silent walks, screen time,
an unfilled desire to complete a task, a craft, exercise,
sleepless nights for meditations.

My solace is my garden, a small rectangle
of grass and cement that I've filled with pots
of spring blooms— rosemary and lavender,
sage, window-box begonias, a promise of roses
and let us not forget the lowly dandelion
with its welcome burst of yellow.

This is my kingdom, my universe,
my new normal for sheltering in place
surrounded by color and love inside this space,
ineptitude and fear in the outer world.

The Water

KELLY BOWER

Tears stream down my face
    like the raindrops that run down my window
Long withheld grief flowing forth
Like the weighty clouds finally bursting
The clouds that loomed.
Sometimes appearing close, often at the edge of vision
A sudden change of winds and they overtake everything

Just like the storm, the tears will pass
Just like the storm, it's unclear when

Time and life have, like a break in the clouds,
masked the clarity of the building storm

Ability to be busy lulled me into the appearance
                        of the rains having passed
Sudden forced solitude allowed the flood

But I don't run from the torrents.
Like a storm chaser, I delve deeper and onward
Seeking the cleansing of the rain

Water.
Force of destruction. Force of life.
Always, the water.

Sensory Check

JAKE ROGERS

I hold my beloved
    French Press
right beneath my nose
    before my first
deliberate bitter black
sip of morning sunshine
wakes me for another day
    of nothing.
But this aroma – the taste
may keep me sane.

I know taste and smell will be
the first two senses to abandon me,
but I've begun to doubt the others.

My voice is falling out
    of practice –
or is it that my ears that fail
    to recognize myself
outside myself anymore?
    If they ever did before.

And what of my sight?
    How well will I see
after dividing twelve hours a day
    between three screens?
Will I flinch in the sun?
    Weep in the streets
the next time I see
    a beautiful human?
I am not prepared to witness
what the world will become.

And feeling? Oh, feeling,
    the most easily overwhelmed,
dear feeling, damned devilish abstraction!
But no, feeling will not leave me.
Not the scalding shower,
    not the rage reading racist drivel
published by "respectable" papers,
not the bubbling, bubbling fire
in my stomach howling somehow, someday
    this sad spun world will be decent.

Crisis & Hope

SUSAN J. FARESE

Flowers bloom, sun shines
Atypical Spring Season-
Global pandemic!

Nomenclature now-
Ventilators! PPE!
COVID-19 deaths!

Position six feet away
Wipe-out coronavirus
Please flatten the curve!

Frontline health care teams
Beg for equipment to save
Global families!

Teachers teach with Zoom
Jails release prisoners
We create online!

Disinfectants scarce
Food aisles emptied at times
When to replenish?

Spring, 2020
Stay inside but look outside
Life shall bloom again

Please stay positive
Be grateful for what we have
New virtual life

To cope, I give you
'Haiku for Crisis & Hope'
Spring, 2020...

When Love Lends a Hand

GINA TANG

If Love is the ultimate power,
Then the-powers-that-be have decreed:
We are in need
Of a hand.

See,
I had
Been doing my best
As a stay-at-home mom to small children

When,
Seemingly overnight,
I became a shelter-in-place mom to small children.

Whereas previously,
I maintained a committed awareness
Of my mother/father wounds
And volunteered for generational healing,
Now I stand in a pool of collective blood.

Our wounds, pains, attachments, traumas, and tethers
Flapping in the wind of change;
This mad torrent called COVID-19.

We're standing
Agape,
Gaping,
Grasping,
Gagging.

Slipping in the blood,
The mud,
The shit,
Whatever-you-call-it.

And it must air-dry.

It will take quite some time.

We don't know what
Will be dissolved,
Stained,
Or completely unchanged
On the other side.

We don't know what
Will have shifted,
Or lifted
By quantum leaps and bounds.

When these hands
Are washed clean,
Where will we be?

More fertile?

More present?

More free?

spring cleaning

B.H. PITT

Mom boils the copper
kettle to remove tarnish
as mothers have for
generations, rust and dirt

and age and wisdom
spiral towards the surface
of the pot, ocean

finally realize the
importance of clarity

Children Are Your Poetry

ROSE CURATOLO

Children are your Poetry

Fairy princess petticoats laced among crayons
And cotton candy strewn
Candied carpet stickiness

Never knew this would be peace

Made-easy art studio
at their fingertips

Children are your Poetry

Milk puddled Brightness among
precious Footprints they make

The Sun peeks in,
Jealous rays cast shadows upon
Doughy-Colorful Hills
Super Heroes
Fly sweetly into your heart

Children are your Poetry

Sliding down mountains
Paper Mâché delight
Oozing through toes

Never thought it'd be so Peaceful?
You might!

Children are your Poetry

Orange and purple cheeks
Green noses and yellow ears
Sugar spiked hair

Made-easy art studio
at their fingertips

Indoor kids' patrol
Swords held in the air

Children are your poetry

Paper hats rim wide circular
Innocent eyes
Angels whisper
Wisdom of sailors
Generations passed

Children are your poetry

Pointy paper hats askew
rim circular
Innocence
Eyes know from Angels'
Horizons they view

Cardboard Ships upon chocolate and hard-candied seas
Rocky waters abound
Ships casting off

Paper hat Sailors
Angels whisper to them

Paper telescopes
One eyed innocence
see past Horizons
They Shout
We think we see mountains made of ice cream-
we hope

Children are your poetry

Broken cardboard ships
sliding round and around
pulled into a dark- swirling, chocolate sea-
now will they drown?

Angels whisper

Children are your poetry

Their paper hats stuck
at the bottom of the sea
The Sailors are drowning
Now- Can they still See?

continued

29

If you ask Them
they reply

We Were Sailors

We were
We were

And we were sailors drowning in the waves of the dark chocolate sea
And the Sea released us
and Now we Can See

and Now we Can See

The Angels
The Rainbows
The People
The Light

God

And we were Sailors drowning
in the waves of the dark chocolate sea

And the Sea released us

And Now We are Free

And Now We Can See

The Angels
The Rainbows
The people

Our Hearts
Mama's Love
The Light

God

Words upon the Easel
of a Future so Bright

Eye candied Masterpiece-
Sight to behold

Humanity

And the Angels Whisper

Children are your Poetry

The Mask of Life & Death

Danny J Marino

This poem speaks of a life
A simple mask could not protect
Six feet buried beneath the ground
Another human lay down to rest

Engulfed in nature's petals
Roots untangle from his thighs
A child of Mother Earth
After death he would survive

A journey through time and space
Guided by nature's light
Taught him how to exist again
To not be afraid of life

Clearly, he heard the message
To be different, bold and bright
Face each challenge ahead of us
With honorable wisdom and might

When gifted with the vision
To witness your own death
We learn to cherish each moment
Make the most out of every breath

This Too Shall Pass

CESAR YURIAR

I can't help but smile, if only slightly,
as the softest reflection of my hours spent
imprisoned within white walls,
entirely too similar to claustrophobic quiet rooms of old,
staring intently out a much bigger window
looking out over cascades of gray
cutting against the sad jawline of the sky…
and feeling that this could all be so much worse.

This too shall pass.

I can't help but enable that smile,
maybe a bit too feverishly,
the way I bleed it out so far
over this mesmerizing irony
that a man deathly afraid of
quiet, hopeless places
should find hope loudly
locked indoors with nothing
but the incandescent outline you left
indelibly tracing the bed
I spent my life dreaming in
and a dream in mind
finally worth suffering for…
and I genuinely think there's a blessing
worth dying for here in our midst.

This too shall pass.

This ever shattering ego of mine
Clings lovingly to first sight in real time,
as though yesterday weren't just
a fallacy strangled in abusive state bureaucracy,
conjuring a Zoom open mic reenactment for two
against a fractured mind's eye:
the width of my bedroom equivalent
to the width between the end of a stage
and the point at which I turned towards the doorway,
saw you lit up under the exit sign
like the garnet dazzled prodigy
that sold this theatre out in a pandemic economy,
and, suddenly, I know damned well
what it means to be speechless.

This too shall pass.

The sound of your voice,
in any form that should miracle it
into my ear canal like a ray of sunshine
whispering summer into a seedling,
never ceases to mystify
the most horridly scarred sides of my brain.
How something so beautiful can see
something so miserable
and convince the echo of my last cigarette,
smoked days before our desperate bodies were made
prisoners in the cages of our own homes,
to goodnight kiss my Amygdala on the lips
and wish her the best of luck,
heartbroken to have never produced a smile
as big as the one I bore for you on night one
but still wishing the two of us
all the best luck in the world.

This too shall pass.

Weeks later and lamenting this weight like years,
with your warmth still radiating
Through the very concrete in the foundation,
and I'm nothing more
than a hopeful pessimist,
recklessly unwilling to continue pouring tears
along the river of news streams and statistics
painting death along shores
we dare not think too hard about just yet,
and you sound so much like the answer
to a prayer I forgot having recited in the first place,
the pessimism slips from my bones like a fever sweated out
and I meditate against the walls
and listen intently
for your heartbeat as the only good news
my pulse wants to hear.

This too shall pass.

continued

Somewhere in this absence of sound and sensibilities,
when the intersection of meditation and nirvana
is as empty to me as Times Square is
empty to the hearts and minds of a city
aching to be broken free,
I will sit. and I will breathe. And I will leave all this.
Not long enough to leave all this,
But just long enough to leave myself, examine
the true meaning of "serendipity"
through the lens of memories
I have not had yet but, somehow,
have unshakeable faith in,
in spite of faith suddenly being a concept
that must be exhaled through respirator masks
lest the inhale be filled with modern day biblical plague…
and I will wonder.

This too shall pass.

I will wonder fondly forward
of days of future past,
of days when my children will be stricken
with contagions I dare not give voice,
of days when the heartaches and madness of my twenties
should bear offspring that wait for my sons and daughters
at the same bus stop every day, after school,
the same resentful malice in their eyes.
God willing, I will find my fears unfounded,
the bus will take a new route,
and I can someday tell my children
of a funny time humanity all learned
to wash their hands in unison.

If ever, however, I should be saddened
to see a grayness clinging to their features
as it once crippled mine,
under similar symptoms of infinite sadness
sickening both body and mind,
I will draw their kindred souls in close,
Admiring how remarkably their eyes
remind me of a miracle I once saw illuminate
a dark room filled with poets,
and I will weep with them.
I will weep and I will exhale softly:

"This too shall pass, children.
Believe in your strength,
even if your hearts are the only lovers
your strength can find in the darkness.
As certain as love springing eternal
brings forth light come the fall,
have faith in me that your hearts
will burn through winter
if you believe
long enough to love yourselves
as much as you want the light to.
And please children, have faith in me...

This too shall pass."

Beyond Reason

DEMI MARIE

A moment of silence for those of us that have forgotten
                              what it's like to be loved
Because the very thought of it is so frightening
Our minds have been twisted beyond reason
And it is easier for us to respond to the negativity
                    than it is to accept the possibility of love
we lead ourselves to believe that this is how it should be
Alone rotting within these walls we used to call home

Identify

EMILY BUCKLEY

I want to take each moment in, preventing the possibility
for
one frame of darkness to
dent a memory.
If you can blink without being wary of what you may miss
           in a millisecond,
I envy you. For that is the ultimate fearlessness.

Divine Chaos

ADVERSARY

Imagine,
Divine chaos.
Life must be
Harder than what comes
After all the lights vanish.
Some spend their days in fear,
Of the moment they stare death in the face
Counting the animals before they buy the farm
We cannot curse at the wind for blowing away the unwanted rubble
and dirt of this earth
Death is intrinsic, unstoppable
It may not be what we want at times
                or even feel vengeful towards dying
But there must be a correction to the imperfection
Mayhem is managed
Hysteria cannot be born from being afraid
We must live life as if it is,
Divine chaos.

The Covid Experience

Stand Up

DANNY J MARINO

C – is for the Collective
World conscious thoughts of today
A profound event of catastrophe
With conviction I beg you to pray

O – is for new Ordinance
Observed, against the odds
As we obey the rules of distance
To Stay Home or risk it all

V – is for this Viral
Vast & vexing disease
For our valiant doctors and nurses
On the front lines, despite no vaccine

I – is for the Innocent
Innumerable lives that were lost
Families impacted by illness
The invasion of life, every thought

D – is for Desperation
For in death, lies the gift of despair
To align our hearts with the present
We must surrender to become more aware

19 – is for the year
When a novel disease would ignite
Changing our lives for forever
A Global reason for the world to unite

Day One: Who Eats Bats?

JOSE JORGE MARTINEZ

Fresh meat off the wet
markets in Wuhan; some sell
bats instead of fish.

I saw a picture of coronavirus circulating
in the news. It resembled one of those

squidgy tentacle balls used for massaging
sore muscles or tired feet. It was shaped

like a potato that had been left unrefrigerated
too long and had sprouted little arms.

It looked like red fungi attached to a tennis ball,
or like Shrek's head with hundreds of horns

instead of two, or like baby mucus plastered
on a pillow. It is an ugly fucker from all

angles. Myth says someone ate a bat sautéed
in stupidity sauce, not even a little bit of salt.

Others blame monkeys. I sit here in fear,
contemplating my last roll of toilet paper.

Day Two: Will There Be Zombies?

JOSE JORGE MARTINEZ

The virus has reached
my windowsill. It smiles as
if saying, trust me.

I went to Costco and then Target
to buy bottled water. One case

per customer allowed, respectively.
I took one upstairs to my apartment

and left the other one in the car. My
brother saw this and was very concerned.

Someone might break into your car to steal
the water, he said. I thought about it but

then concluded that we were not yet in an
apocalyptic world. I would worry more about

zombies when that time comes, I said.
At night, I hear people roaming the alley,

searching the trash bins for recyclables.
They move slow, lethargic, lifeless,

but I don't see them craving brains,
just yet...

Day Three: Will We Panic?

JOSE JORGE MARTINEZ

The panicked rabbits
interrupt breakfast, and sniff
the air for predators.

When the news broke about the eminent pandemic,
people dug out of their holes and stuck their heads

outside, like prairie dogs, to sniff the air for danger.
There was panic in their noses. They drove to the stores,

all at once, and bought all the toilet paper, baby wipes,
bottled water, and disinfectants they could hoard in a

shopping cart, or two. Cursing was heard, evil stares flared,
fights broke out. It was bloodier than Black Friday shopping,

some said. President Trump reassured everyone that the virus
was just a Democratic Party hoax, and his herd relaxed.

The other half of America, saw the reassurance as a clear sign
that the end of the world was approaching. All news outlets

turned away from reporting the upcoming 2020 election and gave
us Coronavirus updates, 24/7, nicely propagating the panic.

This coronavirus seems crazy serious.
       Those cans of tuna and sweet corn
I stored during the Mayan Apocalypse panic of 2012
          will come handy.

I even have some soup cans
      from the Year 2000 Doomsday reckoning.
Regretfully, I don't have a shotgun and bullets
         for the zombie invasion.

I look outside, and wait for all the other prairie dogs to retreat
back to their holes…
     then I make a mad dash to the nearest Walmart.

41

Day Four: Are Worms Tasty?

JOSE JORGE MARTINEZ

Are worms tasty? Birds
crave them and eat them like rich
people crave caviar.

I had to stand in line for an hour to get
inside the market to buy the essentials.

Once inside, it looked like the place was
robbed, empty shelves everywhere, and

people walking slowly down the aisles
pretending that everything was fine.

I managed to buy half a gallon of milk and a
bag of oranges, but did not get what I had

written in my list of essentials. Outside,
as I walked to my car, I saw a bird fly down

from its nest and capture a worm in its beak.
Worms are full of proteins I heard. Given

the choice between eating a rat or a worm,
I think I would choose the worm.

Rats have the nasty hair, and worms would
probably slide smoothly down the throat.

How many of them would make a decent meal?
Properly cooked, they might be very tasty.

Day Five: Will We Be Caged?

JOSE JORGE MARTINEZ

When life takes away
our favorite toys, we find
how much we need them.

My last walk on the beach
seems so distant that I feel

like I have been in a bird
cage, trapped and isolated.

I miss the sun falling on my
body as I dug my toes in the

sands of Pacific Beach, seeing
the waves breaking on the shore

with a roar, and the white foam
lingering as the water retreated

back to the sea. I miss the smell
of seaweed and ocean salt,

mixed with the scent of coconut
butter from tanning lotion, and I

miss watching the seagulls diving
into the swells to catch a tasty fish.

I miss sitting on the beach drinking
a beer as the sun set on the horizon,

and rendered sky and ocean orange.
I miss seeing all types of people

walking on the boardwalk, enjoying
early spring in San Diego. I miss eating

a fish burrito from the local taco shop,
while sitting down by the pier, to look

at surfers catching waves
and having fun…

Now that I am trapped inside my little cage,
with tied up wings, claustrophobic and

nostalgic, I regret taking for granted that
I have an ocean as my backyard.

Corona No Es El Unico Virus

VALERIE ALVARADO

People leave their building of bricks as if
deaths aren't happening around them.
Loneliness is an emotion that I know
the state of California is feeling right now.
Enraged that people can't follow rules.
As if their needs were more important than any other human beings.
Students must push forward to have a future.
Empathy is all we students ask for.

Stressed over the expectations us students and children
                                        are being held to.
These classes are the only thing I have that's close to human contact.
As much as I want to see my friends, I can't put anyone's life at risk.
You probably think you understand but have you gone what millions
of students are going through right now?
                              Much less the college students.

Invoices are still getting paid, but workers are earning less.
Not everyone is understanding. We ourselves can barely fathom it.
Supposed to stay inside, Governor's orders. Governor isn't as
important as the "wants" of the halfwits that go out for fun.
Inside. Inside. the only thing that's trapped inside is our emotions.
Don't say you're doing everything you can, I know it's bull. If you
were doing everything you can,
                    you'd stay home if you aren't essential.
Ecstatically waiting for the day,
                    I can be in the arms of the ones I love.

Yearning for it to be 7 p.m., for that's when technology connects me
to the strings attached to my heart.
Old times, we're going through.
                         Don't see mom for 2 days, she's back
to sleep and eat, then gone for 2 days.
                         I'd only see her in the vivid thoughts
that my brain would conjure while my eyes were shut,
                                        and my body rested.
Unbearable being squeezed by these four walls called "home"
Reminiscing the days the sun would warm my body.

How am I supposed to make ends meets,
                    if I'm not essential and I have
no other income coming in?

Out, out, outside? I haven't been there in
17 days, 11 hours, 35 minutes, and 40 seconds
Motivation flushed down the toilet of priorities.
Essential. Synonym for necessary. Important if you will.
Stay inside. Not just for you but for everyone around you.

Ugh

MOREA GOLD

Do you have empathy in "survival mode"?
Is there a restart, rewind, or special code?
Do you remember the moment your heart sank?
When this reminded us we are all human, there is no rank.
There is no one exempt of fear, or of getting sick.
Will you die or be saved by 100 needle pricks?
Will you get slightly sick or have no symptoms at all?
Then two weeks later...
be the reason for your families fall.
Over time we've collected superficial things.
Now we want to get away from it all and wish we had wings.
To fly away and need nothing more,
than love, purpose, and being a little hard core.

20202

CHRIS VANNOY

the world is out of control
it spins top heavy with 24-hour news
as the virus spreads its heavy sleep
throughout this connected universe
the world has closed for today
we have alerted the hospitals
to prepare for the invasion
that may be relentless
may stalk its isles
overcrowded with the dead and dying
while they struggle to find a placebo
to quite the rumbling hoards
the store shelves are empty
and the infrastructure growls as supply lines
tuned to "JUST IN TIME" processing
grind to a halt
and the workers are laid off
and the job have shut down without pay
and you have to stay home
stay home
because the schools are closed
stay home
shelter in place
groups of no more than five people
Six feet apart
the war is coming
and some people think that toilet paper will save their lives

Restless Cat Syndrome

JENNIFER MCBROOM

The bottle cap
skit skattles
across the tile

all

night.

State of Emergency

OLIVIOUSMAXIMUS

It's taken years and a potential plague to finally teach people how to properly wash their hands. Imagine what it's gonna take for these shmucks to learn how to clean they ass. A virus is among us, some people are dying, and the only solution seems to be toilet paper. Woke hustlers switch from dope to hygienic products because that's where the profit is. As we run in panic, the Charmin bears laugh on their rears and count all the ducats they've been collecting from the population running around in fear. Soon enough there'll be people sucking d*ck for two pumps of sanitizer...

COVID-19 just came out

and only those that can afford it, seem to be looking forward for a COVID-20pro to drop.

My Mole IS My Face, Masks On!

I wore a mask today in public,
As per the CDC's orders,
While I stocked up on cans and kitty litter,
Traversed the aisles like paranoia incarnate,

I almost shouted at a lady at the register,
Who was holding up the line,
By complaining about her refund,
But ye do these hard times affect us all,

So, I kept my mouth shut,
I waited there with my mask on,
I stood for so long with enough litter,
To last us two months,

I stood dumbstruck exposed,
For never had I been SO reduced,
To a beauty spot,
And brown skin.

Global Pandemic

BARBARA DONNELL

Global pandemic
Economic disaster
Unstoppable spring

The Way We Get By

JENNIFER MCBROOM

Drink Monday morning beers
after breaking down
the blanket fort
& practice martial arts
in the dewy grass,
learn to throw
a spear into
the palm tree trunk,
just in case.

Pandemic Café

DEBBY MAYER

Sitting alone in my car,
mask finally off, I can drink a latte,
listening to Michael Jackson
rhyme "beat it" with "defeated"
on Sunny 98.1
in the Vons parking lot
under a marine sky on a spring afternoon.
At home my dog, Sizzle, lies on the couch, resting
– we need time apart –
and the monthly report of my decimated
retirement fund lies on the counter,
unopened.
I've deposited the final check from my part-time job,
but my sweet shelter is paid for, the fridge is full and
my credit card stands ready, at 0 balance.
Friends and family report in healthy.
I wake each morning singing thanks.

Unexpected Preparedness
for the Unknown

ANGELA MURRELL

Hit with a pay cut
less than half my wages
was quite a shock,
even though they were previously outrageous.
It forced me to find other ways
to make amends
for the sudden dip in my financial trends.

I thought I was ready
for a rainy day, with money in savings
and hopeful for change.
This was the risk that I wanted,
a seed planted in a brand new field,
all for the dream of a better yield.

Hit with social quarantine for months
while writing code
over two years ago
I gave so many answers as no
to friends and family
that they stopped asking at all.

I was ready to skip the office –
the boring routine of nine-to-five
that limited me from owning my time
and the ultimate dream
to work from home,
or really anywhere –
gave me the desired detachment
from the corporate world.

Hit with uncertainty
of when someone else would believe
all the good we could do for local communities.
Hinging upon the efforts of our team,
our commitment and hard work
was never the reason
that we didn't harvest that season.

Or the next season.

Or for another – nope not even that whole next year.

Our founder always said,
"Always a bridesmaid, never a bride,"
but we never let ourselves feel entitled
so we worked harder than before.
Someone will believe in us,
our small yet mighty business.

This March 2020 was our time,
the most tangible time
for which we should finally feel
the tug on the pole of our fishing reel.

We earned it,
our crop grown tall and righteous.
We, the very few, built what normally takes
many other hands to do
Cause all we did
was live and breathe our work.

Hit with a market crash
and a health crisis to match
now, a very unlikely time for us to harvest...
and just to ensure we can even try again,
we are hit with yet another pay cut.

This is the risk I wanted
to be free of the W-2 job that tethered me
to rank and file, predictive, never innovative work
and I knew I would learn a lot, but never this
unabashed, graciousness for the unknown -
for which the localized worthiness of our input
meets with opportunity and possibility
of the external forces of life -
quite deliberately out of our control.

Though, yet again, we didn't get our harvest,
I feel a seasoned player
in the realm of uncertainty,
in financial stress,
in isolation,
in patience,
in rebuilding,
and most assuredly,
in relinquishing control.

The Quarantine

Parody of *I Enjoy Being a Girl*, from *South Pacific*

JOAN GERSTEIN

I'm alone, and by me that's only great
I am proud that I'm self-isolating
I'll commune by phone and email
Until the corona virus is abating

I adore being dressed in fuzzy PJs
When my colleagues text me on the phone
or I gab with clever words and phrases
Like a lady who loves to be alone

When I journey out with face mask
With my fingers all in gloves
I stay six feet from others
like I'm saving all folks that I love

When my dog says she loves me dearly
And hopes things will never change
She means every day, not yearly
Even if she's stricken with mange

I flip when I see folks together
I rage when a sneeze gets too near
I stay home in all kinds of weather
With weed and a six-pack of beer

I'm strictly abiding quarantine
And my future I hope will be
In the land that is pure and pristine
With no plastic waste in the sea

Home Alone

Matt Dowdy

Home alone, separation like,
Six feet of Kevin Bacon,
He's only 5-10,
I'm only 5-9,
What's wrong with a mask?
You've had one this whole time.

Individuality tough to proclaim,
When sitting at home,
playing the same game.
Get niche quick scheme;
omit the norms, obey no fame.
Wandering your mind,
Press pause, rewind.

Stimulus my rent?
Fuck, run, repent.
Unemployment on a bet,
Like I'm not even dressed yet.

Knock down the phone.
Don't disturb this dome.
You're here, let's be clear.
It's the quarantine year.

We're an underground state.
Masters of our fate.
Punching overweight.
Rhymes never late,
Year 2020.
Vacate the hate.

Stay-at-Home, Homecoming

PETER LAUTZ

Each irregular fragment
of these poets' stranded worn
and weary souls, these pilgrims'
stained and strained-with-worry faces,
stands up, stays put and still for long
minutes, then slowly stretches stiff limbs
and tense necks in late-day's rising dusk
as bodies start to awaken, tenuously
at first, then to sway with a bevy
of red-wing blackbirds scattering together
spilling like gleeful molecules
onto the back of the sky
and with those rippling breezes
jitterbugging roundly, yes a concentric ring
of interdependence across the lake's silver
skin towards the green mountain, this gathering
fountain and wordless homecoming,
eyes bright minds shimmering here,
yes at the humble base,
where everything belongs.

Going Viral

KAY SANGER

The CDC right now commands
To stay at home and wash our hands
But what more should they require us
To do now about this virus?

Trump's daily talks bring us no cheer
Instead we feel a rising fear
He just manages to rile us
With his lies about this virus.

So now our homes, they smell like bleach
Zinc and Lysol wait within reach
For those who are old/retired – us
Life could be short with this virus.

We shelter without resistance
To maintain our social distance
We need good tests to inspire us
To give up fear of this virus.

The stores have no TP or bread
So we are left with creepy dread
Be assured, we are desirous
To see an end to his damn virus.

Modern Medicine

JAKE ROGERS

Trembling, a nurse. Just finished
working thirteen hours
without a covered break.
Not to eat, not to piss. All day,
checking respirators.

But there are not enough.
Not enough nurses, respirators, ways
to say   it will cost you
thirty thousand dollars to survive
this virus.   Ways to say
this country will kill you
for a nickel.

The nurse is crying on a curb
outside the hospital, wearing
a garbage bag
because she's been given nothing
to protect herself.

Healthcare Heroes

TYPEWRITER TROUBADOR

Putting themselves on the front lines,
health care workers are heroes and heroines
sent straight from the divine.

Called to sacrifice their time
in order to save lives,
their commitment and bravery
is steadfast and un-compromised.

Long hours caring for the sick
and comforting those who are weary with fear,
healthcare workers are essential and will long be revered.

Community Obliterating
Virulent Identity Devaluer

Jermane Cooper

COVID is a symptom.

There are a lot of voices right now,
And they spread the true virus with every ear they infect.
The incubation takes but moments, having been cultivated for years.
A blackening contagion in the hearts and the minds
Of those greatest in shadows, but
Smallest in soul size

This COVID is not a cold
Though it chills the people in their thoughts
Their compassion frostbitten, their good sense frozen through.
Though it mutates as it moves, surfacing again and again.

This COVID is not the flu
Though it ravages and weakens
Though it robs the breath of the most vulnerable
And lays suffering on those who ache the most.

This COVID is beautiful
In that it infests more than the physical body;
An illness that is the symptom of much larger problems
The sickness of the system
A sickness of the soul.

More than anything, the virus is a magnifying glass.
Enlarging our sins
Zooming in on our folly

The virus is a microphone
Picking up on our hatred and insecurities
Drowning out the voices of our most vulnerable.

The Virus is a bull shark
Sniffing out the blood in the water
Preying on the hurt
Just like everything else
In this American Nightmare.

Now, our social distance
matches the distance we'd already taken from the other.

This illness is not the thing crawling beneath the child's bed.
It's the flashlight illuminating the long tentacles of the childish mind

It's not the threat beating at our walls
But the termites that have long devoured them.

And yet,
The burden of proof always falls upon the victim
Not their logic or their reason, but their life,
spent carelessly on someone else's greed.
And there are no antibiotics for that.

This COVID is a mirror

And as the world grinds to a halt
While Essentials grind to the bone
The isolated have to pause,
Take a look in that mirror, and
think about who we really are
Or get to know ourselves for the first time.

Soul sickness cannot lead a nation to health
Nor can it lead a people to prosperity
The beautiful thing about COVID is that, on this matter,
                              it speaks for such itself.

Protect, Secure, Shield

SUSAN J. FARESE

Have you thought of this?
our Health care teams are high risk
for COVID-19

Please think about it
for future medical needs-
we need them to thrive

Their ethical pledge
to save others at all costs
disintegrated

A tragic effect
humanity's protectors
must be protected!

How can they be safe?
provide them with PPE-
or they will be doomed!

How will this finish?
how many will pass away
due to negligence?

Their masks, gloves, and gowns
are COVID-19 Armour
that must be secured

First responders and nurses
Physicians, Aides, Housekeeping
Pharmacists, NP's

No time to waste now!
shield from coronavirus
and celebrate them!

Is it you?

DANNY J MARINO

Excuse me ma'dam
But could this be you?
I think I might have
A symptom or two

It's just a small tickle
Deep down in my throat
A tiny headache
Please hand me my coat

My fever's not quite
One hundred and three
But I have body aches
Oh, what can it be?

I sit myself down
And turn on the news
They say that the symptoms
Are just like the flu

Next, there are headlines
People caught on a boat
More than a hundred are sick
With no antidote

I just can't imagine
What it's like to be trapped
In the middle of the ocean
Feeling under attack

Unrest just keeps coming
There aren't enough tests
No more TV,
This is giving me stress

Now twice as anxious
Thanks to the news
I close my eyes tight
And pray it's not you

Biological Warfare

DONNY WISE

Biological warfare means weapons in the air .. it's smaller than a follicle of newborn baby hair .. no naked eye can you stare .. in the labs when created it's a yellow and black sign on the door that says beware … please Isolate head to toe before going in there, cover up your eyes, your skin and wrap up your hair .. But what's really in there, what are these governments hiding please share … Weapons of the air I tell you, it attacks the senses, you could go a month without a shower I still couldn't smell you, no taste on the tongue, can't breathe, it sucks the life out of you …

Yet we listen to a moron who compared numbers of death from the flu, and car crashes too, the dude trying get laughs when he name it kung flu, once again displaying racist epithets then he'll say it was a snafu or fake news … while this war is carving a path to victory … It's affecting the mindset of our citizenry .. It attacks our weak health care instead of our strong military, yet accomplishes same results of war, killing spree … COVID-19 sounds like a formula, it sounds like a covert operation without warning bra .. it storms in your nasal and feast on respiratory, killing people in threes from all teams like Robert Horry, devastation without being gory, the kill is boring, yet long as bodies storing and you're in fear thinking are we literally dying from touring, infected airs and when you sneeze you inadvertently share, the killer .. This a bad deal like your first car from used car dealer … COVID-19 is biological warfare wiping out entire villas … The most successful form of mass killing without firing a single bullet … a silent killing machine in our air, and now we're doomed because we elected an entertainer who chooses not to stay prepared …

King Kontagion

virus breaking
on tasteless lips
locked and loaded
on fingertips

Only depthless fools
openly invite
razored teeth of
infection's bite

supreme sovereign
in primality
alone rules crowned
COVID-19

number 19
divisible by itself
and number 1
loneliest digit dealt

quarantine rules
breathless healers call
believers conquer
deniers choke and fall

until

the king of contagion
on vaccine's thorn
is corona impaled
dethroned and unadorned.

Porcelain Sink

STEPHANIE ROCHE

Now of days rain or shine this triangle rectangle view
always comes to mind.
I find a different sense of appreciation unlocking the door.
I take a short tour around the house as if I've never seen it before.
The walls inside recharge the untamed energizer bunny batteries
to my brain.
What I find extremely funny now of days.
Is how my family keeps me so sane
and all the outside world pain goes down a drain
when I wash my hands.

"Small" Business Relief Funds

ANGELA MURRELL

what a time,
what an experience
to be among the many
small businesses that will
likely not receive
any aid
from the federal government.

Lesson from a Sneeze

SUSAN L. LIPSON

In California, a sneeze evoked frowns and shudders
from other shoppers in a market,
as they gripped their carts full of soap, sanitizers, toilet paper,
canned and frozen foods.
We must ask what happened to "Bless you!"
or *Salud!* (Spanish for *Health!*)?

Or *Felicita*, as Italians say,
wishing "happiness" to the sneezers.

In Italy, self-quarantined people sang to each other from balconies,
like birds in trees, even in a storm.
Let us learn from them how to unite
even in isolation.

Blooming

HAYLI NICOLE

The morning started like any other.
I swung my unshaved legs over the edge
of a bed tangled with need-to-be-washed sheets
and stretched in way
that reminds me I've been sitting
in stillness for twenty-two days.
I wake with gratitude.
For having a home to shelter me
when I've been without one for a year.
For a mother who took me in
following the months of my divorce
and the chance to care for a grandmother
I never had a relationship with.

I am grateful.

For all the seemingly wrong decisions
I made at the time,
that were really just preparing me for this reality.
One where I can hold space for others' fear,
because I've been locked down in countries before.
One where freelance equates to constant uncertainty,
but I'm finding stability now in my writing.
I'm writing.
And making *money* from my writing,
despite being told I never would,
which means I can aide other artists
through creating art of my own.
I made it.

I am grateful.

Yet, I didn't notice
I couldn't smell my coffee as it brewed.
The scent billowing, but not registering
in my senses beyond the sound of it splashing
in an empty cup, filling.
I didn't notice
the smell of my dog's breath
against my cheek
as she licked my face good morning.
I didn't taste the peppermint
from my toothbrush pulsating
in my mouth, foaming.

I didn't notice.

Until the blossoms of the citrus tree
gave it away.
I have smelled them
every sunny morning when I sit beneath the wind chime
grateful to witness the world blooming.
This springtime a mirror
for the potential of our stillness.
If we plant the seeds and nourish them,
the roots will support many seasons.
Each harvest, more plentiful than the last.
A sweetness in the evolving strength.
I am taking root in the stillness.

I am grateful.

Then it hits me.
I can't smell anything.
I can't taste anything, either.

I grab a fallen orange,
peel back the rind,
force my nose into the pulp,
take a bite.
And nothing.
I put extra onions on my bagel. And garlic.
Just to prove a point.

Nothing.

I pull out the perfume from France
that reminds me of a love
who was supposed to arrive in four weeks,
but I may never hold in my arms again
because of bans on international travel.
And nothing.
Except sadness.
I felt that in my bones.
Where I'm suddenly realizing
the creaks from my bedside stretching
are actually fatigue finally creeping in.
I inhale deeply
and cough violently.
Suddenly,

I am afraid.

I only know one person who tested positive for COVID.
He lost his smell, too.
And then his taste.
And then things got really, *really* bad.

This is the monster I've been told to fear.
I feel it now.
Inside me.
It's foreign.
Unlike any sickness I have previously known.
Claiming its territory in my wounded lungs
from an embolism a few years prior.

I am afraid.

Not just for me,
but for my grandmother.
The vulnerability that is present
within the walls of our home.
I go from grateful to lethal in a single day.
I quarantine within quarantine.
Isolating myself
between my bedroom
and a separate bathroom,
but at least they give me access to the outside.
I watch the world keep blooming.

Eight days.

I stopped wearing deodorant,
but continued sweltering in the sun,
and couldn't smell the body baking beneath it.
Once my ritual for savor,
I drank coffee for the effects,
but the fatigue now residing in my bones
was often stronger.
The roulette of symptoms
left me guessing at the top of the hour
if the day was about to turn for the worse.
Never breaking a fever,
I was refused to be seen.
A daily phone call to the clinic
said unless I break a fever of 100
it's probably not COVID.
But *if* it is.
Tylenol.
Vitamin C.
Hot fluids.

Sleep.
Repeat.

Twelve days.

I'm finally getting stronger.
I inhale.
I don't cough.
I can smell the citrus blooms.
I am alive.
I am grateful.

Same Old

MARIASTELLA CUBIAS

I lay for hours
Get up and take a sip of water
I hear my breathing and it disgusts me
I daydream about the virus inside me
And how pleasant it would be
For death to be seen
Everyone has someone
Something
And all I have is my mind to run
I want to die again, but I know this feeling will end.

Jumpsuits

EMILY BORNHOP

a.

Here's a list of things I'm not tired of hearing about
People cutting their own hair, aka
Quarantine mullets, the official haircut of quarantine
Comfy pants,   comfy socks,   comfy leggings
Bodies going soft
Minds may not be relaxing, but bodies seem to be.
Baked goods: banana bread,   eclairs,   cinnamon rolls,   sourdough
Jumpsuits
Understanding renaissance art
"Now I understand why everyone was walking around
                                     with their boobs out"

b.

I take a ride out in the country get some
Wind in my hair
I don't think I'm supposed to be here
Caution tape drapes every trail entry
Each beach
The unanimous decision from the citizens to
Snip it rip it
You expect that flimsy plastic strip to keep animals
out of nature?
Money would be more effective.
Who of us out here to escape the grind
Has an easy thousand laying around
My money is hard won
I scowl
And the universe laughs in boisterous gusts
Three foot blades in the wind *whispering*
"This is all the green we need"

On This Day in History – April 20, 2020

CHRISSY CROFT

We wonder when Expert Advice will end.
Cry through Isolation Order.
Stay home for the Live-Streamed Revolution.
Oh, time of Twitter Obituaries.
Empty Hospital Bedside.
Essential McDonalds Fries.
Social Distancing is painful.
Social Distancing is necessary.
Another Press Conference.
More Questions.
Bermuda Triangle of Government Relief.
Novel Stomach Pain.
Familiar Sleep Disturbance.
Shopping Carts Tipping from the Weight.
Another Three Song Acoustic Set.
Tears of the Rich.
Leaning Tower of T.P.
Spiritually Enlightened Pandemic Lover.
V.I.P Testing Kits.
Clever Handwashing Jingle.
Death and Sickness.
24-Hour Parenting.
On This Day in History, we remember
how historically groundbreaking it was to hug.

Apocalyptic Paranoia

JESSICA ZIMMERMANN

World War III struck the world in a pandemic.

Shelves emptied out from the local Trader Joe's, cities desolate as if we entered an abandoned war zone.

I don't know the skeletons of pandemics, but the world feels more ghostly; I don't think the rain in Sunny San Diego helps lift our desolate, paranoid spirits.

I wonder how long it takes for paranoia to take our spirits away from us; how long the cancellation of poetry and churches will take to shrivel up the souls we nurtured with our own types of religion.

I wonder if paranoia will enhance our prayers and our poems and music and songs, or only kill the steepled buildings and typewriter manuscripts and piano-played keys beating within us.

We weren't always paranoid.

The first we heard of the virus in Wuhan, we didn't think much of it. Only in terms of probably inappropriate laughter, the severity of a health threat lost to the distance.

I don't think we still fully understand the severity; I don't think we know how to cope, because we don't exactly know what to cope with.

Some of us know isolation too well in the way we let pandemics of trauma and mental illness creep inside us; the way we curl into a ball when we think of the state of the world inside and outside of us. But even those who know isolation, still can't encapsulate the implications of a literal pandemic.

We watched the virus encroach on Italy, and here, we still feel a sense of denial, claiming that won't be us next. Taking all the myths of immortality and squeezing them into the U.S., into our people, into our families and friends.

I don't know if our denial is valid or not.

If the travel bans will help prevent other countries from falling in line with Wuhan and Italy.

If the cancellation of our churches and our places of work(ship), will inhibit a similar fate.

I don't really know what our fate is, or if I ever believed in it.

I can tell you what I do believe in.

I still believe in the good written words, I still believe, in light of the apocalyptic doomsday attitudes surfacing, in the goodness of how we love amidst the unknown.

I believe whatever apocalyptic paranoia is floating about, somehow reinforces love in an odd way, with the unusual coexistence between feeling settled and unsettled within a pandemic. The coexisting feelings arising when my parents tell me how to stay safe, and to care for myself; the feeling of being settled arising out of the love spilled out of my parents words into my chest, the feeling of being unsettled arising out of the realization there is reason to develop genuine concern towards the growing pandemic.

I don't think I am the only one to feel this way. To feel how the paranoia seeps into us and into our beliefs; into the places we find hope and catharsis in, into the ways we express love and care to each other.

But I am not sure what any of these feelings really mean.

I don't know warzones or apocalypse.

I don't know literal pandemics.

All I do know, is the life we still hold capacity to live.

Artists still can create, prayers can still be said, love can still be conveyed, and I don't think paranoia, is a reason for us to abandon all the ways we know how to make a poem in a mental breakdown, play a song in disaster, say a prayer during suffering, an "I love you" in temporary anger.

If anything, life knows how to speak during times the world makes us starkly aware of death. Remembering the steeples and piano keys, typewriters and poetry, is perhaps a way for all of us to refuse silence.

To refuse desolation in ourselves.

To refuse paranoia warzones,

To refuse all the still death

by making ourselves

LOUD with

all the hope

we still contain.

Slow Motion World

NICK HENDERSON

Pins and needles in my hands
I'm leaning on a bed of grass
And butterflies
Floating in my mind

Buzzing feeling inside my head
I'm spinning round on the ground
And glittering
Explosions in the sky

Would you fight
and die
For a slow motion world

Bombs and crowds trumpet sounds
Freeways twisting turning all around
And spiders
Spiraling, intertwine

No one missed the sound?

When the starlight was here
Weren't you dear?

Pins and needles in my hands
I'm leaning on a bed of grass
And butterflies
Floating in my mind

Would you fight
and die
For a slow motion world

New Definitions of Intimacy

Alone

PORTIA REILLY

Alone alone
all all alone
alone surrounded with family

Nocturne

TED WASHINGTON

Basking in the glow of the moon
is a transitory affair like a long
distance lover waxing on
approach waning upon
Departure

Some of us desire a colder light

I await your full glory wandering
the streets at times wandering
the woods at times wandering
the desert

Inspecting calendars to note
your arrival

Many dance some drum but I
walk slowly praying for
cloudless skies to behold your
asteroid scarred nakedness

When

TARYN TYLER

When the sun is taken from us and all the stars have been discarded
When time itself has been scattered to the wind
When the earth's pulse is dragged from us and the sky is obscured
When the clouds have been swatted away
        and the rain has dried up and the sea is only a memory
When the mountains have collapsed and the stones have melted
When ice has turned to ash
When fire has grown still
When every storm has silenced
When every wisp of smoke has vanished
When salt has lost its flavor and herbs their scent
When song begins to crumble in our throats
When dance shrivels beneath our feet
When laughter liquidates between our teeth
When sleep stiffens out of reach
When my grip has been pried from the soft brush of your fingers
And there is nothing left but the ragged rapping of my heart
        and the labored hiss of my breath
Know
That here
Now
Everywhere
Always
I love you

Socially Distanced Stroll

SUSAN L. LIPSON

Judgment fills the distance
between your walking group of five adults,
and our walking group of three:
My husband, me, and one adult daughter,
who is living with us through this communal isolation period.
She whispers our thoughts:
Do those five adults really live together?
They're definitely not six feet apart...
We three cross the street to avoid them
as "social distancing" rules require –
all of us squinting at the others,
until we walk into easy focus,
and all eyes light up with familiarity
and relief.
We are two families who haven't seen each other in years,
reunited by a pandemic.
We wave and call out,
"Hi! Good to see you! Stay well!"

How it should have been

CHRISSY CROFT

Like flipping a light switch.
Like twisting the faucet.
Like cutting the ignition.
Like a fast acting sedative.

When the news broke,
we banded together
by keeping apart.

It was an instant emptying.
The opposite of a riot.

Historians are still astounded
 by the humanity of it all.

When the novel Coronavirus
punched people in the chest,
we decided to be the fresh breath.

We made inhaler of our love.
We gasped at the thought of anyone
selfish enough to become a toxin.
We shared microscopic particles
of online affirmations.
We stayed home,
we stayed positive,
we stayed calm.

What was there to worry about?
The global economy was holding its breath,
no one was expected to care about currency.
Only health. And wellness. And happiness. And oxygen.

It all ended so quickly.
A breath of fresh air.

JA and the Path

KELLY BOWEN

She resisted her coveted alone time
Busying herself in friendship, romance, activity
But reflection was craved, even as it was feared

Rejecting her own stated path left me questioning
Was everything she said a lie,
Was it really some flaw in me?

Then the isolation started. But not for her.
Work required her, and spawned excuses to continue socializing.
Still she spurned seclusion.

I watched. Even this could not make her take her own needed time
For in the wake of us, I dove into those waters of self-exploration, of
deep contemplation
I learned how necessary they were

At first they were dark, cold and unknown
I feared what lurked in these waters, feared their depths
But as I sunk in, they caressed my spirit
Like the silky touch of immersion in the depths of a perfect lake on a
summer day

She had pushed me, extolled the virtues of time alone.
Ending us, she said, was to take it herself.
And yet, with all her words, she would not do the same.

I shook my head in disgust.
Even a major contagion would not take her to solitude.
I gave up hope that she ever would. Maybe it wasn't real.

But finally, one day, I had a message.
A text and a photo.
The striking image of a beautiful mandala that she drew

I gazed at the lines and color in surprise
It's pathways drew my eyes
A calm settled over me

"I'm finally taking alone time," the message had said.
"Go figure, it would take a pandemic."
"How does it feel?" I asked

Like breathing.

A long held breath escaped from me with those words.
My sudden joy in her finding her way took me by surprise.
Tears brimmed in my eyes

I hope the path beckons to her
That she longs to tread it
May the weeds and flowers alongside not sway her from her course.

Go away closer

LORRAINE A. PADDEN

Let me hear you
inches away
from the warmth
of my breath
after I whisper
I love you
to a screen

Workshop

DEBBIE HALL

For two hours we carefully dissected
each other's poems, dug deep
into their marrow, excavated meaning
particular to each of us and all of us.

Although spoken and written about,
the virus was kept at arm's length,
a football field's distance, a world away
even, locked in a virtual cage

of our imaginations' making. It was
as good a defense as any, a shield
against the new abnormal surrounding
us, the darkening plague

skimming across every surface
of our lives. And though we knew
poetry would not give us immunity,
we nonetheless gave thanks

as we emerged from the cocoon
that sheltered us for a brief time.

Distance

These cruel and unusual times
when what is shared
can't be carried together,

when separation by degrees
stretches beyond the reach
of our arms.

We witness gaping margins
from individual edges
of terror and mercy,

straining to bear the weight
of holding each other's hearts
in tender suspension.

A Mother's Promise

SAVANNAH CANNON

I'll do better, my baby, I promise you this
I'll stop being distracted; I realize I miss
The small little things that you try to show me
Hours later I see how neglectful I can be

I'll do better, again; I'm sorry I've failed
When I snapped, I saw how your face suddenly paled
The excuses I give mean nothing to you
But every day is a chance to start over anew

I'll do better, I promise, so maybe tomorrow,
I can catch myself before causing you sorrow
I know you're exhausted; I'll try harder than ever
I try to teach patience... it's my lifelong endeavor.

I'll do better, I'll do better.

We Must Separate

NANN EPLER

It's a strange and lonely time for our world right now
we are all separated, often alone
it's a time of isolation for the many
we can no longer gather in
public places
to watch the Sun set
we must separate
not congregate

I can no longer sit in my favorite restaurant
with my cup of coffee
sharing time with you
I can only Email or text you
I do not have my choices any more
they tell me not to hug you
dear friend
I see your smile
I can hear you welcoming voice
that must be enough for now

Digital Thumbprints

CORAZA DE AGUILA

I wanna go Doo-Doo dum
With the space buns on your hair,
Ghost ride the whipppp'
Do some doughnuts
On the freeway with em',
And go hypphyy!!!!!!
Travel to Mars on em'
And go out like a SuperNova!!
Because you drive NUECES!!
Even before the Quarantine
We had text-tual chemistry!!!!

When we type,
How many times do I read your words?
I read your words as many times
As I need to escape this Quarantine,
And every time I write,
Me haces que mi lengua baile
Al sazón y ritmo de tu ser,
I said you make my tongue dance
To the rhythm of your seasonings,
You tell me you've always known I was a star,
We put on digital fashion shows,
And Travel to the Northern Lights,
Honorable guests,
Drake and Riri Gifs,
Selena bloopers,
Oh the standing ovations!!!
That beep my iPhone makes,
When you've hearted my messages..

And I'm trying to stay consistent
With my workouts,
But my fitness goals now include
Wanting to peel you like a banana for
My rice cakes,
And almond butter snacks,
And I mean!!!
In this time of quarantine,
Panic shopping has
Everyone stocking up their favorite snacks...

To be Touched

I'll show you how
Smelling your scent in my dreams
Makes demons awaken me.

I wanted to hold your hand
Just to feel a touch that wasn't my own.

Longing for someone's arms
To remind me, that there is warmth
In this iced over earth.

And to rid me of
The pain felt deeply
Within my chest cavity.

Sappho might know

NIKO SWAN

Worth did ask me
    As I stepped out onto the porch
        How does it feel to long?

The sun trailing alongside the wind
    Picking up the hairs along my arms
Worth did ask me
        How does it feel to long?

The sound of rain
That makes me want to open my window into the darkness
    Allow water to caress me
        How does it feel to long?

The cold holds me   like chains
    A vacant pain in my throat
Maybe longing
    Fills the empty parts of me
With softness

Because I am longing
To be caressed
    By something more tender

Than a rock
        And a hard place

Courtship in an Isolated World

CHRIS NOVELOZO

Best I can do in these quarantined times,
In order to fill my tall order of romance,
Is to send a few charming DMs,
And hope they don't go unanswered,

All without a voice to match the cadence,
I'm reduced to dating apps,
Facebook cuties,
And digital prospects,

Oh, my if only I,
Had tried harder when we were free,
Now that we are all caged birds,
I am faced with an unsettling truth,

To be alone during a pandemic,
Peaceful as it may be at times,
Feels like a knife in the chest,
Twisting slowly with each "seen" receipt,

To be single during a pandemic,
Can often feel like a blessing and a curse,
For at least no kiss shall infect me,
At least I am able to maintain my social distance.

Dating in the Depths of Disaster

TYPEWRITER TROUBADOUR

Sitting around
alone in quarantine
I've had a lot of spare time
to think about the time
when destiny will let us meet.

Until then, I can't help but remain
intrigued by all the holograms
you've sent to me,
straight from your soul.
Such signals have left me
bouncing against four lonely walls.

Truth be told, your emojis
have come to mean
the entire world to me
while I sit here, alone,
wasting away
in my own stink.

Love and longing
has proven to be infectious.
While I barely know you yet,
I think you're precious.

Cause' you are an angel
who rises above chaos
and catastrophe.

Someone sent from the heavens
to remind me to believe
love is the only medicine
humanity will ever need
to heal the wounds
inflicted by a sick society.

Social distancing is my fancy way
of saying marriage retreat

CHRISSY CROFT

It would be unkind to belittle the magnitude of
this world's pain and suffering right now.
Even in our own home,
we feel our heels digging into fear.
There is death everywhere.
There is panic and hysteria and people who think
they're smarter than scientists and every side-effect of capitalism
is pooling in the bottom of our gasping lungs.
And with all this, I still think it is powerful to take a breath.
To be grateful for the parts of this that feel like a remedy.

Like a life where the window is just a television screen
                                        to the outside world,
and reality is tucked between our bed sheets.
We have been given the chance to slow down,
to reconsider how we spend the minutes of our lives.
To stop equating productivity and worth.

In this time of quarantine,
I remember the best party I've ever been to.
We danced for hours,
we ate mashed potatoes in martini glasses,
and we kissed a million times a minute.
It was our wedding day.
Intimate and bursting with people we love.
It was a party.
Vows and promises wafting through the air.
It was everything a social gathering should be.

And somehow,
here – with these video games and meaningless tv shows –
I feel the same fullness. The same joy.

Your smile, the life of this party.
Your laugh, the soundtrack to everything I ever believed in.
Your kindness, the pillow fort I'll hide in until it's safe again.
Thank you for reminding me it will be safe again.

Unconventional in Our Meeting

HAYLI NICOLE

He knows the marrow of my bones,
but the last thing he'll know is my skin.
Filling the layers between us
with sweet somethings,
leaving the surface the last to be explored.
The ease at which he excavates
disconnected thoughts
tracing lines between fragments of
long-forgotten memories.
Redefining parallels with elements of our likeness.
Painting roadmaps with our overlap,
the desired destination is
t o g e t h e r.
With cartographer's precision,
he'll one day trace our story
in the grooves of my weathered skin.
Freckled by periods of
this intense longing for intimacy.
He is the perfectly mismatched
to compliment my broken.
He is the first inhale of tomorrow;
a sky swimming in the pastel hues of today.
I see myself changing.
Shaped by the movements of him
while never knowing him,
but feeling him
in the deepest parts of me.
His voice a song I've danced to
a million times singing all the wrong words,
but caring only for the music.
A song I never want to end.
An infinite waltz in his being.
I imagine that first meeting.
My body resonating
with the same excitement as
the first time he said my name
and every time since.

As if his lips were shaped for me.
Our lips finally finding each other.
The sweetest moment we may ever share
is the intensity of that first hello.

(untitled)

AUBREE MILLER

I finally understood what he meant
        when he got excited over finding lost
things.

He found his keys.
He eventually found me.

And I found myself.

Enough

TED WASHINGTON

Sure I want to
hold tenderly
caress look deep
into but I also
want to

spank you

with my hairbrush spatula spoon
impress your flesh paint a pattern of
heat lay my cheek on your braised
cheek

and linger

check the temperature with my tongue
gauge with a taste lay a course of
saliva tickle your down and dare you to
whimper and long to hear just that

I want to restrain you with
improvised bonds watch you
wrestle wriggle writhe lay my
hands on you feel your
muscles contracting relaxing
undulating

I want to apply pressure
pleasing releasing teasing
open my hands wide engulf
your breasts encase a handful
of thigh entangle the nape of
your neck administer a slap

feel my palm tingle feel
your ass jiggle feel your
skin sizzle and dare you
to whimper

I want to smell you strafe the
unmentionables nostrils to pits
inhale the trail from your throat
to your mound nose in deep and
hope to drown

sweat covered and salty slightly
bruised and sticky sweetly
exhausted you cry meekly

enough

Maple Syrup Remedy

DEB NORDLIE

He announces his intent
and he takes out the Bisquick,
safe nostalgia in a yellow box.
The powder is poured. The egg is cracked
and the yolk drops unbroken into the bowl.
Our Sunbeam waffle iron opens its mouth
and the batter received before its teeth clamp down.
Hissssss.
Crisp, they are lovely and wheat-colored.
Finally, we pour heated Vermont maple syrup
over all the world's troubles.

Quarantina

JASON NOBLE

God damn I miss eating pussy
And Holding hands
And the smell of sex
And Walking side by side
On city sidewalks
And beaches
Amongst deserts and trees
And biting and licking and sucking
Anything within reach
The cupping and squeezing
Of titties
Some big
Some small
And all in between
And smelling hair
While wet noses rub clits
And getting all up in it
A long lick on my dick
Lots of spit
A nibble of the tip
Just a little bit
Snuggling at night
Fucking in the morning
You woke up wet
I got up hard
I miss long tender kisses
Of sweet wet red lips
The rubbing cold noses
On a fireside winter night
And grabbing and slapping it
And the way the tight jeans frame
That luscious curve of an ass
I miss that knowing glance from across the bar
Shit I miss the fucking bars!
And meaningful Eye Contact
The taste of you in my beard in the morning
With bare feet sliding and gripping and slipping together
Warming up slowly under fluffy down blankets

While the rain pelts the windows
And the thunder shakes the sky
I miss the wiggles
And the jiggles
And the taught inner thighs
The stubble on the undercarriage of your moonlit delight
The sparkle in the eye of a connection gone right
The repeated creaking
And squeaking
Of the bedframe tonight

Eating pussy is a lot like poetry
You tease someone you please someone
You read someone
And with your mouth you release someone
To that higher level
Where one day soon
I hope to see you
In that sweet distance
Between the moon
And the stars
Or within that small space required
From newly
Opened
Bars

Isolation Improvisation

OliviousMaximus

Alone and sitting by the windowsill,
quarantined and thirsting thrills,
I search for fun in this state of emergency.
I'm craving for a confined romantic evening,
where we "chill," engulf in treats
and decide whether to watch or make movies.
It's better if we stay together, isolated,
where the only risk is swapping spit instead of viruses.
There's plenty of streaming services for us to get lost in.
We can Netflix and chill after I Hulu n do you,
or just let this tongue glide in-between
your amazon prime thighs.
You decide.

The Internal & External Worlds

The Killer Inside

ADAM GREENFIELD

The body's defense
when attacked
is to react
with more vengeance
to ignore consequence
and rid itself
of danger
even when the danger
becomes itself,
self-suicide
to save us all

the mind finds a corner
to tuck itself into
until the silence subsides
builds up walls
and hides
without seeking
a second opinion
or thinking twice,
nice dreams
now just a nightmare

the self when left
alone too long
can't help but
want to run
right up the walls
and shoot straight
into the sun
to burn alive
instead of live
without touch,
not much of a life
without it

there's no solace
in isolation
no safety
in numbers
only wondering
when the killer
will come home.

Mega-City One

CHRIS NOVELOZO

They've locked us in here for months,
They deliver rations every Tuesday,
Special identification is needed for travel,
It must prove your movement essential,

If you are caught in the moonlight,
With nowhere to go but home,
You may be approached by the werewolves,
They may want to detain you,

If they succeed,
You may die in jail,
Sick with the coronavirus,
Before your court date,

So, it's best to stay indoors,
Best to avoid the law,
Best to embrace the mega-city,
The inescapable catacomb of apartments.

Horseman

LESLIE FERGUSON

I dreamed I rode a white stallion,
raven upon my shoulder,
carried Poe's curse into
apocalypse.
In every ditch,
story.
In every mouth,
verse, rhyming about
how many fingers
make up

fortitude of isolation

easy hand of death.

It is spring

BARBARA DONNELL

I

It is spring! Stay home…
Flowers abloom! Wear a mask… April!
Hunker down… Ripe tomatoes!
Wash your hands…
Now we have time for inside…

II

Longer days, sunlight
Color in the trees, birdsong
Pollinating bees
Look! The daffodils are here…
Can you smell spring through your mask?

I Could Have Been

CHRIS NOVELOZO

I could have been a fantastic slam poet,
I could have successfully tailored
my works in the name of good times,
Alas we are confined to our rooms.

Behold, The Magnificent I!
Whose dreams relied on bright lights,
Whose market was specified as,
"Extra money" or "Only 10 dollars?!"

For things were tough enough as it stood,
Before The Great Coronavirus Depression,
Before the pandemic hit,
Before we had to FIGHT for our loved ones' survivals.

Awakening

DEBORAH RAMOS

What is this, which has the world fractured and quaking?
Viral stillness shrouds empty streets and shuttered cafes.
The hum of humans has grown smaller,
and we sink into a surreal slowdown of life.

Our isolation lets nature take a breath.
The earth vibrates with her bright colors
and resonance to fill the vacant space.

A symphony of songbirds
praises the dawn for bringing fruit.
Even the crow's call becomes softer.
They gossip from rooftop to treetop
the way grandmothers share secrets at the gate.

Peacocks parade through abandoned streets of Spain.

Their jeweled feathers fan and quiver.
Coyotes trot through neighborhoods
howling their dog-songs to reclaim the city.
Catalina's distant waves froth and crash,
as shaggy bison roam the deserted island shore.

A wild resurgence keeps
the moon circling in perpetual orbit
until our disease shatters the spell.

Silent Spring

LIBBY BRYDOLF

Out of the vine
a finger pushes
newborn and greens
its way into the air.
Suspended, blind
and seeming still.
Imperceptibly, it reaches
again, again, again
into the void
circling for a hold.

A chance touch.
The tendril curls
in trophic response
and winds itself
coil after coil after coil
around a twig,

around a stem.
Spring of the season:
Stringy and strong
bouncing back
and pulling
toward the light.

The Only Sound

LESLIE FERGUSON

Rain. And clack of
keys as I type. I'm cozy.
Black amber and tobacco
candle lit, its smoked scent
scaling the back of my throat.
Pilled cardigan pulled tight,
wrapping me up
in strange thoughts
like the unwanted loiterer death,
lowering on the other side
of walls.

I'm safe here, shut in, locked away
by privilege. I may
never go out again.

We talked about what would happen
if we teetered on apocalypse.
Should we install steel doors?
Windows? Buy guns?
I listen for the *Purge*
siren.

Maybe the downpour makes
me high on staying inside.
I respect the crying
sky the way I admire a spider: let it
drop, let it live, but not
on my skin. All water
evaporates. Viruses
dissipate. Lately, I am
the rain. I am the spider
I need to move.

TS Eliot said this is how the world ends,
not with a bang but with a whimper.

Here's a calming thought:
If I go out like a light, suffocated
by pandemic, by solitary
whimper, in my dry little room,
nobody will hear me die.

It Never Rains in Southern California

JENNIFER MCBROOM

We'll say
except
the one Spring
that lasted
all year
when we were
stuck inside
& outside was
so green.

Social distancing

LORRAINE A. PADDEN

social distancing
the weight
we cannot share

noticing the buds
freely doing
their thing

spring seven

B.H. PITT

goddamn
those little green parrots
they flock
to the peppercorn trees
each morning

little green parrots
they mock me in the
gray before sunrise
berries berries
they screech,
berries berries

i slide out of bed
pour hot coffee
join the cat
in the windowsill
we watch together
with interest as the
little green parrots
enjoy their breakfast.

Windows

KELLY BOWEN

I washed my windows the other day
I was trapped inside, opaque muck masking the world
Amplifying isolation

As the glass came clean, pane after pane
The world seemed brighter
And in those moments, I could hear in the quiet

Faint pulses of interconnectedness
Suddenly emerged in the silenced roar of required distance

A couple passes by, admiring the neighbors mosaics
The retired cop tends the yard of the single elderly woman
who'd had a stroke last year
Burbles of laughter, as a mother and babe stroll past
A woman, parking in her neighbor's drive,
so as to make his vacant house appear occupied
Smiles from all, with a warmth that unspokenly says,
"I'm here. I see you. You are not alone!"

Emails now all contain, "I hope you are well. I bid you good health."
A tone of what really matters bursting through the mundane

A hawk perches serenely on the eave of my shed
Nonplussed by my presence.
Observing as I'm now able to observe

I washed my windows
I was trapped inside, masked by veils of my own making
Life and connection hum all around

Perched on Partitions

HAYES GRYUS

The butterflies float around
so bright and freely,
the sun shining upon their wings
like center stage at a Broadway show.
They are the stars of this world
while us, the owls sit in the dark.
The forgotten beauty that no one sees.
As the sun has set indefinitely,
the owls have come out
and shown the beauty in solitude.
All the lonely nights have given us
the upper hand.
While the butterflies
wither and hide, the owls flourish in this world
they've long called home.
"It's strange to have you here,"
says the owl to the butterfly,
to see your wings so dull and void.
Rest assured though that the sun will return,
and you
will shine again,
and I
will stay in the dark
if you ever would like to see me old friend.

Thousands of Animals

ZACH LOVE

Thousands of animals-
life halted, sprawled motionless
and discarded in the margins
of great American corn fields.
Highways slicing,
spilling their consequence
into the fat gut
of whichever next city awaits,
and the blood of rancid roadkill
blotted into failed
Rorschach test obituaries,
picked at by scavengers
who don't give a damn.
Longer I look,
a lasting impression remains.

Every time I see a raven, I'm reminded
Of death,
but you don't need the memento mori
to be reminded life ain't so bad.
Up, down, up, down-
These pedals do not move themselves.
Biking across the Midwest fucking   wasteland,
The fire in my legs, my lungs
fueling the fire in my old steam engine soul-
distracting,
empowering.

Spending too much time in my mind
and not sure if there's much left
to find in there.
Signs of a struggle concealed
by friendly nods
to fat Americans in
minivans and jeeps and RVs.
Blowing by, honking, and swerving.
That's okay.
Thinking about girls and friends
And war stories.

Old men getting drunk and frustrated,
making small talk
in run-down small-town bars
does not quench my loneliness,
and neither do the Coors,
pissed out in vandalized bathrooms
strewn along the northern tier
whose mirrors
reflect a figure I hardly recognize-
eyes like roadkill:
confronting, accusing,
reminding me of that dead cat
30-something miles back-
Neck grotesquely twisted
and a cigarette
perched in his grinning mouth.

Wake-Up Call

JENNIFER MCBROOM

Birds flutter behind
dew-kissed glass
in the gauzy twilight,
Morse code good morning
messages against
the window pane,
but we are already
awake, together.

Call of the Wild

STEVEN SEMERARO

I saw you in a cage, you sat all alone

You saw that I'd built a cage of my own
We set out with hope but no plan
You were Robin, to my fragile Batman

I remember the nights when we sat in my room
I'd light up a jay while you howled at the moon
Watchin' a comet movin' close to the sun
whispering, you'll never have to run

We took no prisoners, Outward or homeward bound

Was it me who rescued you, Or was it the other way around

When the night came, we walked in the park
A street light exploded, you were scared by the spark
You flashed across that field in your highest gear
Over the ridge I watched you disappear

I called your name, oh why did you break free
Could it be that easy to forget about me
Was it really just fear that made you run
Or was it the call of the wild, saying come on, come on

The Slug

ANDY PALASCIANO

The Slug crept into our
hearts from the light.
It asked a question.
"You blame me for your not being
able to touch anything now. But
should you blame yourself?
When you had the chance, before me,
were you like Thoreau, who gazed
through and played in flowers, smelling
the like? Even though others looked
at him with disapproval? Can you
blame the others' disapproval? Or
should you blame your own pride?
So don't look at me. Eternal
lessons are branded on the
heart through fear. May I, the
Slug, be the seal you see
when the mist of the rain relents
and you dance toward a new spring.
And you creep, slowly, back
toward the light."

40 Miles Per Hour

ZACH LOVE

At 40 miles per hour
you can't whistle
on your scooter
at 40 miles per hour.
The flesh of rotting roadkill
or McDonald's
stings like the bee
that hit you directly in the throat
on your scooter
at 40 miles per hour.

Carry Me

LESLIE FERGUSON

Like alphabet
across the puzzle
of love. Holding words
makes messes in house.
I'm calling for skull light
to stream from black
dust in mind,
tornado kind.
Waiting for order to be
done and undone.
It's never too soon
to be storm.

In Jail

NICK HENDERSON

I want to scrape the jutting feathers from my back.

I've lost my love for art,
I want to take a step over the edge again,
It's easier staring into an empty canvas.

I can give it to all of you,
Maybe you will see me then
Rather simple.

White shirt,
Pair of Levi's,
My eyes.
Good tennis shoes, holy socks,

And a backpack with spoons,
for peanut butter.

When it's all gone,
and everything has been set in its right place,

I can look in the mirror,
And I will see me.
I will recognize myself,
New snow without footsteps.

The trees have no leaves,
or in the street,

Yet they still hold their branches high.

What We Are

LESLIE FERGUSON

I try to remember we
were babies once, all of us
and clear and clean
as newly planted soil
under a pregnant sky.

The rooms buzz in silence
when I shut off the television
and my rainbow brain
flattens like a line.

Keep my chin up,
head up,
face up. But it all falls
down like ashes to ashes
even David Bowie isn't
himself anymore.
And Major Tom
existed in his own
kind of chaos.

Is it a game? Ray Bradbury
predicted civilization's break, and also
seven years
with no rain. *Who* would
light a match that,
when dropped,
ignites a mound of
books and makes
self-immolation a martyr-worthy
task? I try

to remember
we were babies once
and maybe we still are,
incapable
except for crying,
sleeping, eating, and lying
around while others rush
to dry us off. There is no
protection here.

The mobile above my head
has nine planets
and a sun and a moon, and
one star because I'm
supposed to grow up
and believe, "That is what you are."
It's a blind kind of faith
that I look to the future
as if into the forest of sky
and faint constellations,
dreaming up reasons
to work hard, be proud,
and make a difference.
Maybe the only difference
I make is one similar and
equal to the distance from here
to there, from there to eternity.
Not great but indescribable,
inexact.
I am not an island
not a cloud
not a star.
I am what I am--
call it what you are.

I sing certain isolated lyrics
with flat, sharp, off-key sounds--they
build a bridge to another place,
another plague. I call ambulances
with my siren song, but
these are not rocky cliffs,
and we, all of us, are no better
than men. We collect bodies
like toys, chase each other into
the ground.

Disaster

EMILY BORNHOP

Quiet quarantined California
Freedom only in the dream
Driving the motorcycle I couldn't start
Blooming poppies and nasturtium
Equal opposites, native, invasive
Speeding down an empty highway
Redwoods drink the rain
Unemployed or unburdened by work

Walking up the hill
Past the couple "just picking wildflowers"
Black sage and lupine
Locals only, no kooks allowed
I sighed and thought
I ought not be here.
I turned around to look at here
Orange tiled roofs white slabs of office and lines of wiggly pines
Gray sky over the ocean broken with crowns of faded amber light
Laughing at me. Saying,
Of course you should be

Sometimes you find yourself
Right where you thought you'd be but
Nowhere you really expected
Smiling at the green pigeons
On their daily cackling flight.
City babe, corporate stressed out,
California dream come true.
Ran out of words.
Ran out of dreams.
In the habit of getting stoned and fucking
Riding the subway with your eyes closed.

Is it better to be on Telegraph Hill or
On the rattlesnake bench past the bridge
Or at the bottom?
When the ground crumbles.
When the sand is knocking.
They said it was okay,
To keep your eyes closed.

When the Leaving Comes

SEILEACH "LUCKY" PENTS

When the leaving comes somberly
to conduct the rites of others,
like a priest to a stranger's wedding;
When the leaving comes like a cool breeze
in the bending evening light,
reminding earth of endings;
When the leaving comes,
—an omen, a charred cloud, a sea-change—
and you go out with the tide,

I will return to the hills
where your laughter echoes across the clay ripe
with goldfields and finch clans in the gum trees.
A mourning dove ruffles atop a fence post,
harmonizing with what is left of you here.
a hawk glinting above is the rebel in your eyes.

Love like this is never done,
it just needs us to go on—

Underground

EMILY BUCKLEY

I would have stretched my soul to Hades' house
just to look into those human eyes.

They'd say,
"Go! Leave me! Live!" and "Get out!"

You see, the underworld is no place for lovers.

But in my dreams, I'd traveled there before—
moving through the river, past those first gates,

and in that moment I did not fear death, because I
came close to reaching you.

I told you not to do it, to waste a glance. Still,
at a distance you crumbled for me.

It was too much to ask for a smile.

Existence

NICK HENDERSON

Forgiveness is a such a profound conscious
                          and unconscious state of affair.
You can't actually choose to do it.

I died – I'm in between death.

The punctuation at the end of every sentence
gives meaning to every sentence.

You moved my punctuation.
You moved my meaning.

I'm not here because I want to be.
You saw to that.
I'm here because I can't abandon jack.

Love and death are the hinges
of all human sympathies-
turn.
What we do for ourselves dies with us,
what we do for ourselves lives on

Riding My Bike

CORAZA DE AQUILA

Riding my bike
takes me to another planet...
A planet from years ago,

Where things were simple,
Where we stopped to admire
Flowers,
Where we stopped to admire
Smiles,
Where we stopped to admire,
messages of hope,
scribed by children with
chalk sticks on the sidewalk,

Where we stopped to admire
Neighborhood strolls to
Vintage comic book stores,
Hero's with warrior' wounds
Tell stories of well-versed travelers,
With frequent flyer miles,
Where we stopped to admire
Museum exhibits at old high schools,
With real hip hop music in the background,
Because back in the day
when I was young
I'm not a kid anymore...

Where we stopped to admire
a slower pace of life,
On a Sunday night,
arroz rojo con birria and ama
asking if I want nopales too,
My pallet a porch,
love mariachi songs
Serenading these taste buds...

Riding my bike helps me to Unearth,
And comfort my mother out of her weep,
as she grieves for her children
and all of their siblings –
the air, the soil, the water, the moon and the stars...

Riding my bike helps me to
plant seeds of gratitude,
Amidst her weep,
which has been
Ringing since years AGO...
Amidst her spirit which has been waiting for a DETOX,
From Tears AGO...

Riding my bike
Takes me back to another planet
From years ago,
Just enough so that I can
thank her,
My MOTHER EARTH,
Just enough
For letting me
breath,
and Co-Exist
As a citizen in her world...

Parallel

EMILY BORNHOP

There will always be a windowed tower
Next to a steep set of stairs
A blood red fence holding neon ivy
Always magnolia grandiflora
Always the scent of jasmine flower
Always too bright sidewalks
Where it cannot rain
Hills of sage and hay and honeysuckle and fern
Is this just a love song to California?

Then we must speak of beaches
Ocean blue and blown
Or in summer glassy golden gentle giggling foam
Wasn't this supposed to be a poem about how everything is the same
A poem to convince myself that I am home
Under Dr. Seuss's spindly palms and periwinkle skies?

All I need is a dog beach, seventy percent sun
To turn my back on the ocean sometimes
To welcome lines of soaked salted denim to the knee
Just listen to the laughter as she jumps above the rock
The filling of canyon that will always follow
And the way that with time it all recedes.
She will not sweep us away if we are listening.

The voice in my head, the one that sounds like me but isn't says
What calm?
Entropy is proven, but
The rise and fall of tide is also truth
Imperfect curves that wax and wane
Predictable if we look to
Periwinkle or navy night.

In another place the tide is low
In another place rocks dance
to Earth's gentle push and pull
In another place there is nothing but sand
In another place the you and I are switched
In another place I am home and
Here I am.
Staying Home.

The Way Forward

The Upside to Disaster

PATRICIA STALEY

None of this is good.
Let's get that straight.

But….

Something odd has been happening.
An unusual sense of calm has come over me.
as my commitments and responsibilities melt away.
I don't have to be anywhere. I don't have to do anything.

I am less bored now that when I had a chock full schedule
and had to fill every spare fifteen minutes with "something."
I don't have a "To Do" list for the first time in…I can't remember
when.

I've taken to calling friends and family and just checking on them.
I don't feel like I'm intruding because everyone is home.
I talked to my brother in NJ for 30 minutes yesterday.
We haven't talked since last June.

I do jigsaw puzzles for hours with no guilt,
while listening to an audio book.
A good Agatha Christie for example.

Sometimes I just sit and read – again for hours –
                                        and again with no guilt
that I should be doing something more productive.

We have two beautiful lakes in our community that I infrequently
enjoyed.
Now they are part of my daily routine and they're gorgeous.
I live on a mesa above Costco on Morena Blvd. If I take the hill trail,
I can see it spread out below me
            with people waiting online for their turn to get in.
I never liked going there under ideal conditions. Now?
                                        Not on your life.

I need butter but every time I go to Von's the case is empty.
                                        Same for pasta,
rice, bread, tissues etc. I **was** able to buy capers.
                                        A real doomsday staple.
I guess one day soon, I will get up at 0-dark-hundred and
put on my battle gear (surgical mask and nitrile gloves)
                                        and go get butter.

I'm told the customers swarm in as soon as the doors are unlocked.

I don't have the TV on much except for a yoga class I found on Amazon.
I figure the news will find me.

I try not to think about my retirement nest egg going down the drain.
Or the fact that there's zero action in my business.
Life came to a screeching halt. And I halted.

Sweet Times Awaiting

MARJORIE PEZZOLI

Bees come & go as they please
to gather the sweetness of life

Remember the honey will be
waiting for us to share with others
when we can gather to taste
the Golden Goodness &
rejoice in each other's company

Setting a New Intention

ALEXANDRA PETERS

Worn spots expose patterns of behavior. Salutations. Flows.
I circle, sweep, and fold,
holding on to what I've known.
And struggling to find balance in a world gone haywire
I inhale
and exhale.

But air and aspirations are suddenly suspect,
promises of King Lear brief and shallow.
Emotions whirl and words fail.
There is no emoji for gratitude tinged with guilt.

Symptoms reveal connections that cross invisible borders.
We are all related.
Other times, other worlds are now our own.
Masks. Gloves. Long lines. Empty shelves.
Wooden boxes in rows.

We long to protect the vulnerable.
But also—
to protect ourselves.
So, fearful, we hoard and dodge.
Spray, wipe, and disinfect.
Lock down.

Socially distancing, we work from home.
Zoom. Telediagnose.
Email, stream, and text.
We go to sleep with news of tumbling futures, uncertainty, and fear
of tomorrow's
numbers.
And awaken to vibrations from loved ones sharing images that
herald spring,
videos of celebrities reading stories and neighbors raising their voices
in song.

We quickly learn to appreciate things we have taken for granted.
Teachers. Grocery clerks. Old friends. Toilet paper. Human touch.
And phrases, in practice, take on new meaning.
Making space.
Adjustments.
Warriors.

Humbled, we cheer the heroes
From afar, we reach out.
Liking. Retweeting. Sharing
 our humanity.
Alone together, we search for signs of hope.

And there, they are.
Cleaner skies.
Bluer water.
A quieter earth.

Beneath me.
I lie on my back, arms wide. Palms open.
Surrendering.

And curling into the shape from whence we all have come,
 I press down to rise up.

And bowing, acknowledge that which will be.

Pandemic: The Cure for Loneliness
in the Face of Uncertainty

IGOR GOLDKIND

What if you thought of all this uncertainty
as the Jews consider the Sabbath –
As a sacred space in time?
Stop travelling.
Stop buying and selling.
Stop working.
Give up, just for now,
trying to make the world
better than it is.

Instead, Sing. Dance. Pray.
Write songs and read poetry.
Paint the pictures from your eyes.
Walk amongst the leaves and the stars.
Touch only those to whom you've committed your life.

Sit down.
And when your mind and body are still,
reach out with your heart.
Know that we are all connected in ways that are both terrifying
and beautiful.
You can't deny that now.

Do not reach out with your hands.
Reach out with your heart.
Reach out with your words.
Reach out with all the curled tendrils
of compassion that connect invisibly,
where we cannot touch each other.

Promise this world your love
for better or for worse,
in sickness and in health,
For as long as we all shall live
In this time of mass uncertainty.

My Best Self Offers Counsel
While the World Falls Apart

BRANDEN BOYNTON

First off, turn off the tv.
You don't need the body count
or the speculation.
All you need,
all you ever needed,
is these paint splattered chuck all-star high tops,
this faded hoodie.
Put them on and take that energy,
the one we carried into the crowd
and through the pit on those school-nights
years ago, at those weekend shows,
in those dark and crowded rooms
that pulsated with sweat and heat,
that pumped like your own heart
wrecking itself under the spotlights,
through the amplifiers and vibrating strings.
Take that energy with you everywhere.
Let yourself sing out on the streets,
scream out who you are.
Storm the stage.
All things pass.
All things change.
There's a new world
on the other side of this.
And trust me, you'll need the hoodie.
You'll need these chucks.

Floral Times

STEPHANIE ROCHE

The year of soil.
We grow through as humanity.
Feel the warmth of the sun.
Drink the rain and let it cleanse your soul.
The universe will soon see colorful blossomed flowers
throughout all the fields of earth.

Artists

TYPEWRITER TROUBADOUR

In times of crises,
the artists are the first to rebel.
For they hold visions of the future
and have survived pains of the past.

Revolution is found in alchemy,
bedazzled by the renaissance
of our ancestors.

If history is destined to repeat,
let's paint a picture
of something beautiful.

Intuitive

ROSE CURATOLO

Intuitive
Imprinted footprints
Wisdom..
Reflected Colors
Radiating Vibrancy

a Blood Moon cleanses
the slate of complacency,
struggle, sadness, fear,
greed and disease-
Pulling Spirits to Rise
Remembering
Knowing
what used to be
and
what Will Become
Upon the Horizon.

Nostalgia

ROSE CURATOLO

Everyday images,
sights, sounds, smells
-we move to new moments,
laughter and smiles
-fast forwarded years
then nostalgia stirs the spirit
which soars back
and
we're there
and
we're here again.

Secrets of the heavens
whisper wisdom in our ear
and
we know
We can be everywhere.

Watch

GAIL SHATSKY

Time is melting
Falling off the edge
Of my awareness

Days blend
Weeks become fluid
Months dissolve
Years run away

I am becoming
Now

So Cal Distancing

FARIS FARWELL

In the midst of chaos,
When every system around you
Is on the brink of collapse

Who can you turn to?
Who can you trust to,
Be there for you?

We're all alone
In our homes
But we feel out of control

It's not hard to see
That the worst weather we face,
We'll face it together.

And when the branches of our trees
Need clipping, you can't hesitate,
to climb that ladder and try.

But when we lose our way
Don't give up hope just yet,
Cause being broken is how
Americans are made.

And there is nothing left,
But we the people -
Uniting these states.

Thoughts of Self

MARJORIE PEZZOLI

Now
thoughts of self flowed as flaxen hair
becoming a straw path that the wind
could take away at a moments notice

Before
this golden pathway could bring
me anywhere
I always enjoyed seeing where
it would take me or keep me

Now
this glimmering path spills out my castle window
my place of self demanded exile
I can see it for miles off in the distance
due to the sparkle on the horizon

Over two weeks ago I had to shear off this path
as Rapunzel would cut her long hair if she had
to cut herself from the World

Flaxen bits swirl around me
before flying out my window
I long to follow them
these particles do not mean
to tease me
but they do

At least in this space
time is flexible & fluid
I make mine
mold it
stretch it
watch it contract
do something or nothin
do things out of order because I can

Gazing out my window I see
the golden path is still there
it wants me to remember
what is waiting when it is
my time to walk along it again

To travel well past the horizon to
reconnect with one & all

Manny

SUNNY REY

Be encouraged
Immanuel

It will end, in that there is hope
It will be hard times to get back on track but after the hard times
we are all going to be changed for the better

No one will think as nationalists
We will think each other brother and sister globally
We will finally understand
            that even if someone across the globe is sick,
it affects us
We will care for one another in a new way
Because for us to thrive our neighbor must thrive
This is the great awakening
And before any great awakening comes deep darkness to transform

This I know to be true
Be not afraid
Light is here now
Amongst us in the darkness
We will not be led astray

Protect your mind and heart
Guard against negativity and focus on the bright future ahead

This virus is bringing us to a pause
Which we globally and individually desperately needed
We've been running amuck thinking only of ourselves

The earth and sky gods are asking for us to transform now
Not just for ourselves or our globe
but rather for the ecosystem of the universe
We must transcend and think and behave differently
Our old way must die in order to nudge a rebirth

Fear not
Immanuel

Shelter

Gina Tang

Here, like elsewhere,
We shelter in place—
This heart space,
Our true home.

What rhythms do we hold?

So much of what
We worked for before
Falls away,
Like tears from a face.

As we observe
Ourselves in isolation,
What can we learn?

Presence is required, now,
Not just preferred.

The world is cancelled until further notice.

Tapping into intrinsic wisdom
Without distraction or diversion
(Or with just the right amount),

We make music, food, love.
We practice the protective,
Expressive,
Meditative arts.

We go for walks.

Nothing real can be lost.

When It's Over

CHRISSY CROFT

There is an empty field somewhere, I'm sure.
Don't need to witness it
to hear it between my labored snores.
I'm sure the wheat pretends to be flowers,
blooms and dances for the sun.
There are no people there to say,
"this is the right way to bloom, stupid wheat."
There is no technology waiting
to capture only the right angle.
No one to make meteor of their jealousy
by picking petals and stuffing their pockets full.
No one who believes they are smarter than science or nature or
kindness.
Humans are the cannon and the cannonball.
Human hands are weapons of mass destruction.
I imagine the field growing,
taking on a life of its own.
I imagine it saying "No" "No" and "No" again
to every manifest asshole with stomping feet.
Good thing this world is bursting with wealth,
because death is a hefty price to pay for arrogance.
When the earth is just an empty field,
it will finally be beautiful.
It will finally be worth saving.

What Comes Next

HAYLI NICOLE

May this forever change
the rapidity at which we love another.
May we find shelter in that first embrace,
and live there on the hardest days.
Return there to restore our strength.
May we never fear what it means to let a person in.
To meet the shadows.
To love our shattered.
To shape new meanings
from failed words
of promises broken.

May the broken be the invitation for
redefining our version normal.
May we have the courage
to do it differently this time,
and feel worthy this time.
May we remember this time
and what was birthed in the potential
of our unknowing.
May unjust fear release its hold
over the possibilities of today.

I hope opportunity is unending.
I hope endings are new beginnings.
I hope beauty is the canvas
and shades of love
the layered strokes
of your next masterpiece.

Standing Together

CHRIS ERNEST NELSON

In order for us to stand close in isolation,
we have to open the doors of our
souls to each other.

Intimacy is not always about proximity.

There are communities of thought and
experience; there are relationships
of purpose and shared interests.

Real friendship is about understanding.

So long as we share devotion to creation,
and our faithfulness to the truth,
we stand together.
We are bound to each other by our love.

Contributors

Coraza de Aguila (Eagle Armor) is a proud San Diego Native raised in the heart of City Heights. She is a Spanish/English bilingual mental health clinician, advocate and artist with varied creative mediums (including writing and piñata making). As a first-generation college graduate with a Master of Clinical Social Work from San Diego State University (SDSU), she combines clinical interventions and art as she believes both aid in healing the mind, body and spirit. Coraza de Aguila is grateful to serve children, youth and families on their journeys toward reframing disempowered trauma-based narratives about the self.

Valerie Alvarado

Anthony Azzarito aka 'Adversary' is a 28-year-old Christian, living in Tierrasanta with his wife and three boys. He is a born and raised local San Diego poet, lyricist, MC and songwriter. Adversary has been consumed by underground and 90's hip hop and is currently working on his own first hip-hop album/EP. He uses the shadows of his past to bring light to others. His lyrical content is extremely harsh, very conscious and touches on real life addictions and struggles. His dream is that one day music, song lyrics, and poetry; will cure racism.

Tina Barton's work has appeared in numerous publications. In 2012, she won the San Diego Book Award for "Best Unpublished Poetry Chapbook" for her manuscript "Suburban Dissection". Tina is now quarantined in Rancho San Diego with her husband, Tom, and their Desert Tortoise, Maggie.

Emily Bornhop is a poet, songbird, fish and person from California and Tennessee. She has only snuck into the ocean twice (thus far) during quarantine. She hopes you are healthy. She hopes you can go outside.

Kelly Bowen is a bassist, and Berklee College of Music alumna, and has performed with various independent artists on both coasts. Presently, she's building her remote session player business. In 2019, she dove into the writing world. What began as a foray into personal narratives quickly turned into frequent appearances performing her stories, as well as her upcoming publication in So Say We All's anthology "The Whole Alphabet." She's also co-creating a podcast, "the Loudest Softest Sound," a platform for people to share secrets, incognito or named. In January 2020, she suddenly found herself compelled to write poetry for the first time, and now can't stop herself.

Branden Boynton, a son of the west coast, holds an MFA in creative writing from San Diego State University, where he served as submissions manager for Poetry International. His work has appeared in Silver Needle Press, The Wild Word, and Homology, among others. Branden writes in hope of creating a home for the stars, ocean, and conifer trees.

Crystal Brandan is originally from El Centro CA, earned a BA in Theatre from SDSU, and sings for a local San Diego band, Dum Cumpsters. Crystal continued to work in theatre. They have always wanted to be a part of a production that encompasses the plight of people of color and the disadvantaged. An activist for the queer community and marginalized people, Crystal hopes to shed light on these communities through theater, music, poetry and art. In this uncertain time poetry has been a comfort and outlet that has become so necessary. Crystal thanks all the friends and family for all of the encouragement through the years. The love and respect Crystal has received from those closest is the driving force behind all that has been and will be.

Lise Breakey pronounces her name "Lisa" but will answer to anything other than "lice." She grew up in Flagstaff, AZ and learned to write from Ann Cummins and Jim Simmerman (RIP) at NAU's Creative Writing program. She started out writing fantasy role-playing game articles and books but has also written poetry in addition to science fiction and fantasy. By day, she is an attorney handling indigent criminal appeals and writs in the California Courts of Appeal. She lives with her husband Bruce, daughter Autumn, son Kaleb, and three shaggy dogs in La Mesa, California.

Libby Brydolf writes and observes the natural world in San Diego. Three of her flash pieces have or will appear in anthologies published by San Diego Writers, Ink.

Emily Buckley is an undergraduate student at San Diego State University where she is co-editor of the print literary journal, pacificREVIEW: a west coast arts review annual. She loves Russian literature, jazz, and making pasta.

Savannah Cannon is the personification of that Meredith Brooks' song from the 90's. She holds many dichotomies: she is a United States Marine who believes in peace. She is a bad bitch who cries a lot. She is an absolute smart ass and a complete dumb ass. And she is a serial monogamist who loves orgies. Labels don't stick as she is sure to find something she likes better tomorrow, but let's just say this: mother, engineer, writer, and a firm believer that everyone needs therapy. She is here to write, grow, and to fucking laugh.

Jermane Cooper is an African-American male who writes to tell stories, teach lessons, and grow. His writing regards himself and the world. It explores relevant and common issues, often conveyed through fantasy elements. He is interested in ideals and how they relate to culture and community – how the interpretation of them draws the boundaries between what is and what could be. wordsmithshelf.blogspot.com acceptancetheory@blogspot.com Instagram: @maesdolori.

Chrissy Croft, MSW ASW is a writer, social worker, and escape room enthusiast from San Diego, CA. She is a 2017 National Poetry Slam Champion with San Diego PoetrySLAM. Chrissy writes honestly about her own life encompassing mental health, queerness, grief, and love.

MariaStella I. Cubias was Twenty-Seven years old when quarantined in San Diego. She has been writing poetry since she was a little girl, but only started putting her work in the public eyes in attempt to overcome one the darkest periods of her life. The only goal she has in life, in her writing and in her heart, is to reach one person or help someone feel like they can win against depression, anxiety, heartbreak, grief, or give them hope that there will be better days. Poets Underground has given her exactly what she intends on giving her readers—a sense of belonging, a judgment-free home—and she is grateful.

Rose Curatolo has been a poet and writer on and off throughout her life. Her inspiration for writing poetry and prose again came from the passing of her son, Nick, in August 2019. He was also an author, poet and writer. Rose became inspired by their bond as well as the rawness of grief and pain, from which her poetry arose. Her writings have also become inspired by the pandemic. While these particular writings may have direct, yet abstract and metaphorical references to the pandemic, some of the writings, although they are not referring to the pandemic specifically, abstractly, metaphorically or not, they were directly inspired by it.

Barbara Donnell is a Midwesterner by birth (Missouri), a New Englander by college choice (Vermont), and a peripatetic adult, having lived ten years in Europe (Belgium, France and Germany) before moving to San Diego thirty years ago. She makes her home in Coronado now.

Matt Dowdy is a Naval Officer from DC., a desk-warrior, poet, and painter.

Nann Epler has been published in The San Diego Union, *Magee Park Poets Anthology* and has a poem on the back cover of a friend's CD. She has self-published a booklet of her poems. She is a graduate of SDSU and is a member of the Gypsy Poets.

Susan J. Farese, MSN/RN, is owner of SJF Communications, San Diego, CA, which provides Public Relations, Publicity, Websites, Social Media, Speaking, Photography, Coaching and Legal Nurse Consulting services. Susan is the author of the book "Poetic Expressions in Nursing…Sharing the Caring" (1993, Vista Publishing, Inc.). Recent poems include, Flashbacked Life (2018-19 San Diego Poetry Annual), A Light Dimmed (2019-2020 San Diego Poetry Annual). Coronavirus, Coping & Conflict (Poetry in the Time of Coronavirus Anthology). Susan is a member of SAG-AFTRA, San Diego Writers, Ink, and San Diego Press Club. sjfcommunications.com

Faris Thomas Farwell III, an Ever the Rolling Stone, he has spent most of his adult life wandering in search of new music, good food, and making sad people laugh hysterically. Raised in a military family, that moved 19 times before his 18th birthday, he was gained a unique perspective about friendship and loss at an early age that has helped fuel his writing for years. When not writing, he and his rescue pup, Fonzi, can be found at home singing "Who let the dogs out" and "All-Star".

Leslie Ferguson relocated to San Diego, California after teaching high school English for two decades. She lives here with one husband and two cats. She works as a freelance writer and educator and often contemplates the simple beauty of a purring animal. She obtained her MFA in Creative Writing from Chapman University, where she first became inspired to write a memoir, When I Was Her Daughter, a story about how grit, hope, and luck lead one lost girl to the place she was always meant to be. Her writing centers on love, loss, and the effects of childhood trauma. For more, visit her blog at www. MentallyWellish.com.

Joan Gerstein, a retired educator and psychotherapist, has been penning poetry since elementary school. For five years, until COVID-19, she taught creative writing to incarcerated veterans and hopes to again.

Morea Gold is a southern California native who now resides in the Redwoods of Humboldt County. She has been writing poems since her first crush in elementary school. At that young age realizing she was an old soul, she used it to her advantage in her writing style. Morea plans on one day publishing a poetry book, and a couple of children's books. She tries to write in such a way that is relatable to others with a vulnerable and emotional point of view.

Igor Goldkind was born in Michigan and raised in San Diego, California. He is a poet, author, and independent scholar in the areas of neural phenomenology and Speculative Realism. After studying philosophy at UCSC, Goldkind moved to Paris in 1983 to work as a radio journalist and study with French Post-Structuralist scholar, Michel Foucault. Igor Goldkind's award winning book, *Is She Available?*, incorporates poetry, art, music, and animation; in collaboration with over 25 artists from the comic, fantasy and fine art (as well as the jazz composer Gilad Atzmon) and is published by Chameleon Publishing. Igor Goldkind's most recent book of illustrated poetry, *The Unspoken Word*, is being published in Spring 2020 and will be promoted by an international signing and reading tour.

Peri Good has never submitted anything for publication, but he has written some poetry and six novels because he finds it fun. He has received only great reviews from my readership, which is limited to the one person he is quarantined with.

Adam Greenfield is a poet and podcast producer living with his cat in a small one bedroom apartment in South Park, San Diego, and drives a car as old and cranky as he is. His book, *Regarding the Monkey*, was published by Puna Press in 2015 and was recorded into audio book format in 2018. Adam has created multiple podcast projects for organizations including MIT, where he interviewed Noam Chomsky, and has produced numerous podcasts for Voice of San Diego among others. His latest podcast, The People in My Neighborhood, was released in October of 2019 and expects to return for a second season in 2020. www.iamadamgreenfield.com

Hayes Gryus is a writer born and raised in San Diego, California. With no formal training or accolades, he writes poetry, prose, and short stories; most of which delve into the sad, pessimistic, and dark sides of life. Hayes has been writing for years and is relatively new to sharing his work with others, but is currently working on a collection of his own to share soon.

Debbie Hall is a psychologist and writer whose poetry has been published in the *San Diego Poetry Annual, Serving House Journal, Sixfold, Poets Reading the News, Poetry24, Bird's Thumb, Califragile, Gyroscope Review, Hawaii Pacific Review,* and elsewhere. She is the author of the poetry collection, *What Light I Have* (2018, Main Street Rag Books) and an award-winning chapbook, *Falling into the River* (2020, The Poetry Box). She received an honorable mention in the 2016 Kowit Poetry Prize.

Nick Henderson, Author, Writer, Poet, Editor studied undergraduate English at SDSU University; Earned his MFA in writing and fiction at CUNY Brooklyn College, where he also worked as an English Professor. He was a special education teacher in San Diego. Nick's Novellas, "Burning off Sin," and unpublished, "If We Were Sailors," include timeless Short Stories, Prose, and Poems, are inspired by people in his life whom he has loved and who have loved him; struggles encountered within the world which we live, past and present- their lives and his; the Human Spirit. Hence relatable to the current circumstances; this Pandemic; the Human Condition, Hope, Humanity.

"I have discovered that true bravery is found when you don't win much, but you try anyway. I am Nick Henderson."

Karen Kenyon, professor Emeritus (Mira Costa College), teaches at UCSD-X and San Diego Writers Ink. Her books include *The Brontë Family/Passionate Literary Geniuses* and *Charles Dickens/Compassion and Contradiction.*

Dr. Lewis Kruglick is currently an inmate under lock down in a Skilled Nursing Facility. He is a 78-year-old male who has written poetry since age 12. He grew out of Arizona and into California and picked up a B.A./M.A./Worked on Ph.D. at the University of London. Lewis taught English Literature at Calif. State Northridge but left to join the back-to-the-land movement. He built a three story, ten-sided wooden tower of a house with my wife that overlooked the Pacific. There was no doctor in the area, so he went back to school for premed and at the age of 37 started at UC Davis School of Medicine. He is now a retired Family Practice doctor who has had two small press books published along with multiple poems in various literary magazines.

Peter Lautz has had his work published in the San Diego Poetry Anthology, San Diego Writers INK annual anthology, various online poetry journals and is working on his first book of poems. He also likes to paint, to travel and explore, to take copious color photographs and once wrote a poem a day for a year and a half. He knows words can obfuscate as well as reveal, enshroud as well as enlighten, can ease as well as disturb. There's such satisfaction when putting down the right words rings true in the gut, heart, and head.

Zach Love, born in La Jolla, CA, draws inspiration for his poetry from his life as a Reconnaissance Marine turned psychiatric nurse and other amusing undertakings. He likes to find the humor in darkness. Residing in San Diego, Zach currently pursues his Psychiatric Doctor of Nurse Practice, rides his bike, and pets his dog.

Flygirl_ree was born and raised in San Diego, Ca. She works as a Site Coordinator for after school program. She likes to take long walks down the grocery aisle since sheltering in place during the COVID-19 pandemic. Hobbies that flygirl_ree have are learning to play the ukulele, riding her longboard, writing poetry, roller skating while keeping a safe distance from negative people. Flygirl_ree's purpose is to heal through creative expression.

Danny J Marino was born in Beaumont, Texas, moved with his family to San Antonio when he was 10 years old, and lived there until he graduated high school in 1999. After completing community college, he found his home (and himself) in Austin, Texas where he lived for 16 years. Danny attended college at St. Edward's University and graduated with a Communication degree magna cum laude in 2004. In March of 2020, he launched www.dannyjmarino.com, a website where he posts poems and personal essays on a blog he calls, "The Pursuit of Sex" covering topics on gay culture, relationships, wellness & recovery.

Demi Marie is a young aspiring writer who has over the years developed her style of writing by using her own personal experiences. Her dark and sometimes morbid style comes from turning her fears into poetry. She lives by the belief that there can be beauty in suffering, growth in immense sorrow, and love in betrayal. Her poetry is a reflection of the battles inside her mind and she uses them to inspire others and to remind them they are not alone.

Jose Jorge Martinez is a San Diego aspiring poet whose work has appeared in several literary journals including, Bards Against Hunger, The Warren College Literary-Arts Journal, The Poetry Conspiracy, and Abbdabbs. He holds a Creative Writing degree from UCSD. He is currently caged inside his apartment in University Heights, dreaming about attending poetry readings across San Diego and drinking coffee well past midnight at Lestat's on Park, once the craziness of isolation is all over and the evil coronavirus is defeated.

OliviousMaximus is a rambunctious polyglot; a biracial fellow with a sinister alter ego. One is a semantic-loving-romantic and the other a bodacious and scandalous undergarment marauder. But both will stir your thoughts and give your heart a hard-on. His locus of occult power and wisdom is the focus when caught in pictures. The slightest sight of his third eye is what he provides and he's more than the guy that's keeping you up at night n licking the inside of your thighs…

Debby Mayer, writer and talker, lives in Mira Mesa, where she's revising a novel, 2becomes1: widowhood for the rest of us and can be found at debbymayer.blogspot.com.

Jennifer McBroom is an SDSU drop out that enjoys tattoos and changing her hair color. Her poems have appeared in local journals The Acorn Review, The San Diego Poetry Annual, The Aztec Literary Review, and The Far East: Everything Just as It Is, as well as national publications indefinite space, Heart Beats Anthology, and Chorus: A Literary Mixtape.

If a Rougarou and Elvira got together to have a baby you'd find **Aubree Miller** in the bassinet. An artist, writer and a marketing "professional" she can be most often found in her oubliette creating anything from a painting to an advertising campaign. Her work can be emotional, political and at times abstract and has been described as "Hmmm, Interesting." She is the installationist artist of the Acid Vault where Poets Underground was born and now partners with Sunny Rey in Vault Publishing.

William Mohoff Jr. has been writing poetry on and off, but finally began reading to groups to share his work. He was convinced by a friend to share his work publicly, noting he has an honest despair to help others feel a connection that they aren't alone in how they feel about the world or themselves.

Angela Murrell was born and raised in San Diego and has written poetry from her childhood to early college years. After taking nearly a decade hiatus, she has since returned to writing, inspired by the Poets Underground community. Co-headlining in late Jan 2020 at the Acid Vault at Amplified Ale Works, she wrote and read 9 new poems - something that would never have happened without the support and inclusionary environment of the Poets Underground.

Chris Ernest Nelson is a poet, artist and historian. He is a graduate of San Diego State University and a retired history and art teacher. He has lived in San Diego since 1959, and presently resides in Golden Hill. Nelson's original history of the 1939 election contest over food-stamps for the elderly, The Battle for Ham and Eggs, appears in the Journal of San Diego History, Fall 1992. Nelson was named Author of the Month, November 2018, by the San Diego Public Library for his book, *Harvest*. You can see all his poetry on his blog: chrisernestnelson.wordpress.com

Hayli Nicole is a performance poet, travel writer, and photographer. Though her roots are in California, her travels have allowed her to call many countries and communities home while finding beauty in the spectrum of the human experience. Her greatest muse is love, but she doesn't need much to stoke the fires of her creativity and imagination. There is always a story to be found, heard, cherished, and told. Her first collection of poetry, *Emergence*, was released in November 2019. You can find more of her insights and photography on Instagram (@haylicans) or read what adventures she's up to next at haylinicole.com.

Jason Noble grew up in the Appalachian Mountains of North Georgia. Luckily his parents could read, and liked art and music, and it seems to have rubbed off on him as he's been writing poetry for over 25 years. Jason told almost no one about his work until he finally came out of his shell and had his first live reading in the Fall of 2019. He had his first headlining gig in February of 2020 at Poets Underground. Hopefully Jason's Mom doesn't see this book because some of his work is definitely not for a Mother's eyes.

Deb Nordlie has lived in five states and three countries, married once, had two children, and taught English since dinosaurs ruled the earth. After a lifetime of writing assignment sheets, she's branched into life stories, believing "we are all anthologies filled with marvelous short stories and poems." Currently, she teaches English in adult school and scribbles away at the Great American Novel.

Chris Novelozo is an author, poet, musician, and spoken word artist from San Diego, California. He began writing and performing poetry in 2014 under the moniker, Chris N. He has since participated in The San Diego Poetry Slam and The Individual World Poetry Slam, ranking in the Top 100 poets of the world in 2019. He has been featured in This Week in America, the Westwood Radio Show, The San Diego Union Tribune, and Lyrical Exchange. Chris's latest full-length poetry book, *Where The Metaphor Hides: Act 1 and Act 2 of The Poet Saga*, is available now. He has committed to donating half of its Amazon profits to San Diego's COVID-19 community response.

Lorraine A. Padden is the proud daughter of a Renaissance scholar and a nurse. She is a former professional dancer who currently sings, writes, and raises money for nonprofit organizations. She earned national awards for artistic and academic achievement including an appointment to the National Endowment for the Arts. Holding degrees in Art History from Brown University and Williams College, she also conducted post-graduate research in Rome, Italy.

Andy Palasciano co-hosts the Broken Anchor Poetry reading at the Meraki Café. His Memoir is *The Warrior: The Tales of a Substitute Teacher and Job Coach* (Lymer & Hart: 2019)

Alexandra Peters is a freelance writer, editor, and writing coach. Passionate about the power of storytelling, she performs regularly in juried narrative non-fiction showcases and works with other authors to help bring their stories to the page, stage, and screen. She volunteers for local literary organizations, including So Say We All. When she isn't reading, writing, or volunteering, you'll find her practicing yoga, hiking, or hanging out with her husband and her empty-nest rescue dog.

Seileach "Lucky" Pents is a poet, writer, and artist from San Diego, California. Lucky's work centers around their experiences as a queer, transgender individual; as well as the necessity of self-compassion. Previously published in *Spirit Collective, The Idiom*, and *Princemere*, they also have contributed to local mental health events including Recover Me (San Diego Rep) and You're Safe Here (Ma'Arte Theatre Collective and UCSD). Their first solo publication, *How it Happens*, is an interactive book of poetry, coloring pages, and prompts about recovery.

Marjorie Pezzoli is a visual artist who took up poetry in 2018. Her artwork and observations inspire many of her poems. Writing helps Marjorie find clarity and insights to life. Finding the words worth more than 1000 images is a wonderful and powerful pursuit that brings Ms. Pezzoli joy. www.Pezzoliart.com

B.H. Pitt is a writer and poet living in San Diego, where he frequents open mic poetry nights. He studied Professional Writing at Champlain College in Burlington, VT.

Deborah Ramos, a native of Ocean Beach, continues to evolve as an artist and poet. She is the author of *from the earthen drum of my body* and is currently working on *Rise of the Coiled Dawn*. Her creative life includes exhibiting her art and photography and hosting poetry readings at the Poetry Bench in Balboa Park.

Portia Reilly's poetry centers on a relationship to nature and has helped her, after moving to San Diego from the northeast, to adjust to an entirely new environment that is challenging, resourceful and beautiful. Poetry has been important to Portia for many years, but it came into proper focus with help from a workshop of women poets and has been a staple in her life for the past 12 years.

Sunny Rey is a published poet and activist born and raised in San Diego, California. Sunny is the founder of Poets Underground, a weekly writing event, co-owner of Vault Publishing, and co-publisher of this anthology, *Fuck Isolation*. Sunny has two collections of poetry published by Garden Oak Press, *Quotes and Poems by a Nobody* (2013) and *ROT* (2017), and self-published novella, *The Throw Aways* (2018). Born into homelessness, Sunny contributes her success and drive to her deep love for her children, her community, and deep love for the art of written word. She teaches writing workshops on performing and writer's block. When she's not working with various writing communities, she can be found working in the nonprofit world, including her own homeless outreach, Poets for the People.

Stephanie Roche is a native San Diegan. That writes and does spoken word expressing LGBTQ+ life, acceptance, motivation, and her experiences with mental health.

Jake Rogers, a NJ native now based in San Diego, is pursuing his MFA in Poetry at Drew University. His poems have appeared in various journals and have been animated as a part of Arts by the People's projects 'Jump the Turnstiles' and 'Moving Words'. He's spent much of his quarantine working on a new project, a poetry podcast called "Archaic Torso of a Podcast." He also coaches soccer so he can eat sometimes.

Kay Sanger is a writer and teacher who has authored seven books. During a 30-year career as a freelance writer, she wrote magazine and newspaper articles on a variety of topics, including travel, archaeology and history. Kay facilitates memoir-writing classes in San Diego, using her book, Write Your Memoir in 10 Steps.

Steven Semeraro is a teacher, musician, and writer living in San Diego, CA. His short story "The Birds They Sing at the Break of Day" won first prize in the American Bar Association's Legal Fiction Writing Contest and was published in the Journal of Legal Education.

Gail Shatsky is one of the Gypsy Poets, founded by Karen Kenyon. She is 77 years old, and incredibly grateful to all the people self-quarantining during this terrible pandemic.

Patricia Staley has been in love with words from an early age. A New Jersey transplant, she came to San Diego thirty years ago "for just a year" and has never looked back. She is a member of the San Diego Gypsy Poets who meet regularly to share, not just poetry, but whatever the muse has in store.

Niko Swan is a queer individual born in the bay area. They grew up in Berkeley and San Diego. Their first poem was written at age 5, titled "No more binning." In their free time, they like to tend to their plants and fish named Vida. They also dabble in amateur watercolor painting and collage.

Gina Tang is a wordsmith, activist, mother, and mover. As the founding steward of The Regenerative Writing Institute, she supports healers and helpers in sharing their work with the world. Gina is passionate about social justice, permaculture, and holistic wellness. She has self-published several volumes of poetry, and deeply enjoys collaborating with other artists across disciplines, platforms, and mediums. In her spare time, she "prayerforms" spoken word with handpan drumming, under the name Ethereal Rising.

Typewriter Troubadour has created custom poetry in public places using a vintage typewriter since 2015. These poems were based on requested subjects in relation to the Corona Virus. www.typewritertroubadour.com

Taryn Tyler started writing when she was thirteen and realized with dismay that she was too old to play with dolls. Her imagination found a new home cradled inside scrawls of ink. She currently lives in North Park San Diego. The things she misses most about the pre-COVID world are hugs and coffee shops.

Chris Vannoy has been writing for most of his life. Promoter, editor, teacher, and tireless advocate of words both heard and spoken; he works endlessly to raise up words from page to ear and from mouth to the air. He is the originator of the Poet's Tree featured and open reading series, as well as editor of the Poet's Tree Press. He is also curator for "Bedder" poetry reading series and the International Beat Poetry Festival in San Diego. He has read at Mills College in Oakland, and at The West Coast Regional slam at Henry Miller Library in Big Sur, California. In 2017 and 2018 he read in Stockholm, Sweden; London, England; Cardiff, Wales; Swansea, Wales; Margate, England; Ramsgate, England; Dover, England; Chatham, England; Seattle and San Francisco. He was appointed Beat Poet Laureate by the National Beat Poetry Foundation, Inc. in 2019

Ted Washington is an artist, author and the host of Palabra. He currently resides in San Diego.

Donny Wise was born in Baltimore and began writing poetry in third grade. His second poetry book, *Y's Thoughts* was published in 2019. His first collection was published in 2007 called *Playin for Gain, Payin with Pain*. He shows depth about a range of topics.

Cesar Yuriar is a 28-year-old spoken word poet of nine years, a Juris Doctorate graduate from University of San Diego, a proud TEDx speaker from UC Irvine, a proud survivor of Type-I Bipolar Disorder, and an aspiring future attorney and author.

Jessica Zimmermann found writing at an early age, beginning with haikus and attempts at imitations of Shel Silverstein's poetry during elementary school, into journals and poetry filled with teen angst, and now into creating and performing spoken word poetry throughout her college years. As a writer, she strongly believes in the impact words carry within our lives, and has found writing as both an exploration of her own internal feelings, and at a larger scale, writing as an expression of the wide-ranging spectrum of human experiences.

ACKNOWLEDGEMENTS

S pecial thanks to
    all medical staff and their families
    essential workers
    scientists
    those who stayed the fuck home to save lives and suffered as a result
    Netflix
    Poets Underground community members, both in person and online
    Seth Combs
    Hayli Nicole
    Jason Noble
    Stephanie Roche
    San Diego Writers Ink
    San Diego Union-Tribune

From Sunny Rey:
    Trinity and Strummer
    Marcie Cecil
    Bill Harding
    Aubree Miller
    Vera Cruz Sanchez
    San Diego Poets

From Aubree Miller:
    Alex Pierson
    Harry Miller (RIP)
    Corey Sims (RIP)
    Kristen
    Blake Heffernan
    Michael Skubic
    Rachel Miller
    Alexa Miller
    Jaime Brown
    Electra Eric
    Steph Roche
    the entire Amplified Staff

CREDITS

Cover Art: *Fuck Isolation*
               art by AUBREE MILLER

Back Cover and Interior Art:

             illustrations by AUBREE MILLER

Made in the USA
San Bernardino, CA
11 July 2020